MOMENTS
with
BILLY GRAHAM

...America's Preacher
**whose ministry led to
our changed lives**

MOMENTS
WITH
BILLY GRAHAM
...America's Preacher
whose ministry led to
our changed lives

COMPILED AND EDITED BY YVONNE LEHMAN

GRACE PUBLISHING

Scripture quotations marked MSG are taken from *The Message*. Copyright © 1993, 1994, 1995, 1996, 2000, 2001, 2002. Used by permission of NavPress Publishing Group.

Scripture quotations marked NKJV are taken from the *New King James Version*®. Copyright © 1982 by Thomas Nelson. Used by permission. All rights reserved.

Scripture quotations marked NLT are taken from the *Holy Bible, New Living Translation*, copyright © 1996, 2004, 2007, 2013, 2015 by Tyndale House Foundation. Used by permission of Tyndale House Publishers Inc., Carol Stream, Illinois 60188. All rights reserved.

Royalties for this book are donated to Samaritan's Purse.

MOMENTS WITH BILLY GRAHAM
... *America's Preacher* whose ministry led to our changed lives

ISBN-13: 978-1-60495-043-4

Copyright © 2018 by Yvonne Lehman. Published in the USA by Grace Publishing. All rights reserved. No part of this book may be reproduced in any form or by any electronic or mechanical means, including information storage and retrieval systems, without permission in writing, except as provided by USA Copyright law.

From Samaritan's Purse

We so appreciate your donating all royalties to Samaritan's Purse from the sale of the books *Divine Moments, Christmas Moments, Spoken Moments, Precious Precocious Moments, More Christmas Moments, Stupid Moments, Additional Christmas Moments, Loving Moments, Merry Christmas Moments, Cool-inary Moments,* and now, *Moments with Billy Graham* to Samaritan's Purse.

What a blessing that you would think of us! Thank you for your willingness to bless others and bring glory to God through your literary talents. Grace and peace to you.

Their Mission Statement:

Samaritan's Purse is a nondenominational evangelical Christian organization providing spiritual and physical aid to hurting people around the world.

Since 1970, Samaritan's Purse has helped victims of war, poverty, natural disasters, disease, and famine with the purpose of sharing God's love through his son, Jesus Christ.

Go and do likewise
Luke 10:37

You can learn more by visiting their website at
www.samaritanspurse.org.

Dedicated to

First and Foremost — Rev. Dr. Billy Graham

and to
Gigi Graham
for her generous contribution of personal words and photos

and
Grace Publishing publisher,
Terri Kalfas, who saw the beauty
and value of sharing praise in
Divine Moments
Christmas Moments
Precious, Precocious Moments
More Christmas Moments
Stupid Moments
Additional Christmas Moments
Why? Titanic Moments
Loving Moments
Merry Christmas Moments
Cool-inary Moments

and
To the 45 authors who shared 48 stories
for this compilation without compensation
just for the honor of remembering
BILLY GRAHAM
the world's greatest evangelist
and the privilege of being part of the mission work of
Samaritan's Purse,
which receives all the royalties from the sale of these books

Contents

Foreword Gigi Graham 9
1. *America's Preacher* – Yvonne Lehman 11
2. *Not a Normal Day* – Patricia Luellen Nicholas 13
3. *Rainbow Over Rotorua: A Tribute to Billy Graham* –
   Nate Stevens 16
4. *In Everlasting Glory* – Lola De Maci 19
5. *A Little Seed for a Little Girl* – Jayme H. Mansfield 20
6. *The Street Life . . . or Music* – Joseph S. Bonsall 22
7. *A Godly Example for the Rebellious Heart* –
   Diana Leagh Matthews 26
8. *Never the Same* – Andrea Merrell 29
9. *Billy and Dickie Are Good Boys* – Nancy Johnson 31
10. *Forbid Them Not . . .* – Wendy Dellinger 34
11. *It's Polio!* – Max Elliot Anderson 36
12. *I Had to Go!* – Lynn Mosher 41
13. *Worldly Wealth, Godly Wealth* – Gayle Fraser 43
14. *From Depressed to Blessed* – Mary A. Hake 46
15. *Billy's Footsteps* – Lowell Lytle 48
16. *Certainty* – Diane H. Pitts 54
17. *The Last Two Dollars* – Carlene Shuler Brown 56
18. *English 101: Pass or Fail?* – Lydia E. Harris 62
19. *A Hero of Faith* – Amanda Hughes 64
20. *What He Looked Like* – Judith Victoria Hensley 66
21. *Linking Generations with a Chain of Faith* –
    Shirley Brosius 69
22. *Billy Graham Was All In* – Diana Leagh Matthews 72
23. *With a Prayer and a Smile* –
    John Jaruczyk as told to Barb Suiter 75

24. *Thank You, Mr. Graham* – Mary E. McQueen 77
25. *Turning the Knob for Billy* – Vicki H. Moss 81
26. *Reach Out* – Yvonne Lehman 84
27. *The Billy Graham Rule* – Karen Sawyer 86
28. *My Tribute* – Colleen Reece 88
29. *Thirteen Pages* – Tommy Scott Gilmore, III 90
30. *Pray Like Billy* – Cindy Sproles 93
31. *Accept or Reject* – Helen L. Hoover 96
32. *Locked Out!* – Suzy Liggitt 99
33. *Back to the Basics with Billy* – Kim Peterson 101
34. *A Sunday Afternoon* – Roger Bruner 104
35. *One Sunday Morning* – Karen Lynn Nolan 106
36. *Words of Wisdom* – Ann Knowles 109
37. *His Continuing Influence* – Diana Flegal 111
38. *A Special Memory* – Fred Robinson, Jr. 113
39. *Because It Takes More Than Bread* – Beverly Varnado 114
40. *This World Is Not My Home* – Debra DuPree Williams 116
41. *Why the Tears?* – Ann Brubaker Greenleaf Wirtz 118
42. *Lifetime Pursuit* – Audrey Tyler 121
43. *A Servant Leader* – Joann Claypoole 122
44. *Mother's Answer* – Penelope Carlevato 125
45. *Until Then* – Diana Leagh Matthews 128
46. *A Special Sign* – Debbie M. Presnell 131
47. *World Changer* – Dr. Rhett H. Wilson, Sr. 132
48. *Remembering Ruth* – Yvonne Lehman 137
49. *Happy Graduation Billy Graham* – Joye Atkinson 140
About the Authors 141

Foreword

As I sit looking up at Little Piney Cove, where our home was for over sixty years, or pass the sweet little house where I grew up in Montreat, I am flooded with memories.

For most of my life, the memories I have of Daddy consist more of Moments. He was away from home more than sixty percent of the time when I was growing up so the moments we shared when he came home were extra special.

We couldn't wait for the train to pull into the station in Black Mountain. Daddy would step off looking so handsome in his overcoat and hat.

We would run to greet him and he would pick us up in his arms and give each of us a warm hug, then we would watch as he turned his eyes lovingly, longingly toward Mama.

Oh, how thrilled they both were to be together again, although they were keenly aware it would be only days, maybe a couple of weeks, of simple "moments" together before he left again.

But Mama taught us to treasure these "moments." And we did.

I had the joy, for more than seventy-two years, to have precious times with Daddy. Memorable moments that I treasure with all my heart.

I could share many of them with you, but this book is not about me. This book is a collection of "moments" other people from all walks of life, experienced with my daddy. Special moments.

I am privileged now to work at the Billy Graham Training Center at The Cove in Asheville where I hear hundreds of stories from folks who have had some form of encounter with my daddy — some in person, but most who have been touched in one way or another by the message he so faithfully preached.

A message of hope. Shared with hundreds of thousands of people all over the world so that they, too, can have this hope by having a personal relationship with Jesus Christ.

Hearing these stories makes me happy we had a small part in these "defining moments" by willingly sharing him with the world.

Billy at age 17

And I can tell you without any hesitation, that Daddy would say to you today, that having a defining moment with Jesus is much more meaningful and precious than having a "Moment with Billy Graham."

However, now we are going to listen with our hearts to several stories collected and shared by folks who had a special "moment" with my daddy.

May you be blessed.

Gigi Graham

I

AMERICA'S PREACHER

Yvonne Lehman

Since I live in Black Mountain, North Carolina, right down the road from Montreat, where Billy Graham lived, I had the privilege of seeing and hearing him on occasion. He sometimes came to talk with and mingle with the boys at Camp Rockmont for Boys, where I worked.

Frequent comments were, "I saw Billy Graham at the supermarket."

"Billy Graham was at the drug store."

"Billy Graham's in town."

"Billy passed by in that old car and wearing a baseball cap like a regular person."

"Billy's going to speak at . . . preach at . . . ."

On one such of those occasions, more than twenty years ago I took my grandson, John, to the church located on the Montreat College campus, to hear Billy Graham speak. After the service, having sat near the back of the sanctuary, I hurried out the door to the lobby and cornered his friend, who held a camera, and asked him to take a picture of me and John with Billy Graham.

To my surprise, he agreed and instructed me what to do. So, as others were talking and shaking hands, I boldly (or was that impertinently?) stepped up and said, "Could we get our picture taken with you?" I turned my head toward his photographer friend who was standing on the stairs, smiling and ready to *shoot* us.

Billy Graham looked toward his friend, and apparently at peace with the situation, graciously complied with my request. Afterwards, he greeted us (something I should have done first) and talked with little John, who smiled and reacted happily.

Additionally, Billy Graham autographed the picture for us when his friend took it to him.

How amazing! The Reverend Dr. Billy Graham, whom God used so mightily to influence and be revered by the entire world, was yet so gracious, humble and relatable that we, and he, were comfortable with his simply being "Billy."

In this book you'll find stories by people eager to tell of their experiences with Billy Graham. Whether they knew him personally or through his ministry, because of him they came to know the Lord Jesus Christ, or their lives were changed and their faith strengthened.

2

Not a Normal Day

Patricia Luellen Nicholas

Guest Group Event Coordinator at The Cove

February 21, 2018 was a normal Wednesday as I walked into work. Well not quite normal, since I had managed to arrive a few minutes early that day. When I entered a room for morning devotions, I noticed a co-worker, with a strange expression on her face, staring at her phone. I asked her if anything was wrong.

"My brother just texted his condolences at the death of Billy Graham," she said. "Have you heard anything?"

"No, but let's Google it." I pulled out my phone and began searching news web sites, and there it was. The headline confirmed the information. News that we knew we would see *one* day . . . but never really expected the day would come . . . *that* day.

In silence we sat in the devotion room where it was confirmed to us, the staff at the Billy Graham Training Center at The Cove in Asheville, North Carolina. Billy Graham had gone home.

We prayed and cried together that morning — tears and prayers were something we had shared together on many occasions, but this day was not normal. Afterwards, we went our own separate directions to begin our day.

What would have been a normal day suddenly wasn't.

Thursdays, the Training Center, a building that can hold close to 500 people is usually bustling with activity. It's a place where men and women laugh, sing, and share together freely in fellowship. But that Thursday the building was empty and quiet as we, the staff, stood in silent reverence as they brought in the beautiful but simple coffin.

Friday brought activity. First, a private viewing for the family and close, invited friends. Next, the staff lined up and filed into the auditorium, a room normally used for training and worship. For two hours, we worshiped in a different way. We thanked God that Dr. Graham was finally home, in the arms of Jesus. We thanked God that he was reunited with his beloved wife, Ruth.

We shared stories of how he impacted our lives, and of the last time he had visited this special place. Then, after standing in line, it was time for us to walk past where he lay in repose.

I will always be grateful to have had this private time.

Several members of the family stood inside the auditorium as we filed passed. They shook hands and accepted hugs. We tried to offer condolences too, but as much as we wanted to minister to them, they ministered to us.

The next day, we gathered in the Training Center for a private prayer, then moved silently into position, lining the way from the Auditorium to the curb.

I stood outside and waited.

When the doors opened, a rush of wind hit us. It was as if the Holy Spirit, who so obviously lived in that obedient servant of God, was still with him as he took his final journey.

Not a word was spoken until after his coffin was loaded, and the family entered the waiting vehicles and left our presence. Then the singing began. His nurses sang, and our tears freely flowed.

The family and security detail had started their three-hour journey to Charlotte, North Carolina, but there was one problem. They would need their own vehicles after they arrived. The decision was made that several of us at The Cove would make the drive and deliver the cars to them.

We drove the same route as the motorcade, but we were a different type of procession, one that went unnoticed by the people standing, and sitting in parked vehicles, along the roadsides.

We noticed them however, and marveled at the sight. The crowded overpasses were draped with flags, and people held hand-written signs. We were able to experience the outpouring of love from the multitudes as we drove that route. It truly was an amazing sight to see.

With long-range radios we were able to communicate and stay close together. Whenever we passed by a large gathering or something particularly moving (which happened frequently during the entire trip), we couldn't hold back our delight, and shared our thoughts via the radios.

Seeing the sheer volume of people openly expressing their respect, moved me to tears throughout that entire drive. It was a moment in time that I will not forget.

Through experience, I have learned that people grieve in their own unique ways. This day, through this reverent observance, I witnessed true expression of grief and love in family and friends who knew Dr. Graham best; and in those whose lives have been changed forever because of his ministry.

Funeral procession leaving Black Mountain, North Carolina.

3

RAINBOW OVER ROTORUA
A TRIBUTE TO BILLY GRAHAM

Nate Stevens

And life went on . . . .
The day I heard of Billy Graham's passing, I was vacationing in Rotorua, New Zealand — half a world away from Charlotte, North Carolina. While to me it seemed the world's spiritual temperature dropped considerably, people in my vicinity scurried about their normal routines working, vacationing, shopping as usual, little knowing a spiritual giant had quietly slipped to his celestial home. After all, it had been thirty-one years since Billy last held a crusade in New Zealand.

That evening, my wife and I dined at Stratosfare, an incredible restaurant, high on a hill, with huge windows offering magnificent views of the city and lake below. As we ate, we watched rainclouds rumble in, misting half the lush valley in cascading sheets while the other half basked in crisp, evening sunlight. Between these contrasting vistas, God stretched a gorgeous rainbow radiating with vivid hues. I've seen many rainbows, but this one was spectacular. It covered most of

the sky, remaining suspended for most of our dinner. Many fellow diners also snuck to the window for pictures.

The news and scene reminded me of when I sang in the choir for the Billy Graham Crusade in Jacksonville, Florida in 2000. We practiced for weeks in the sanctuary of First Baptist Church — tenors and basses downstairs, altos and sopranos in the balcony — while Cliff Barrows led us through the songs.

On the opening night of the four-day crusade, I excitedly climbed the stadium steps to the choir's reserved seating behind the main platform. I had one of the best seats in the house to observe Billy, Cliff, George Beverly Shea, and the Gaither Vocal Band.

After the usual rounds of stirring music, Billy strode slowly to the stage. Already into his early 80's, he needed a chair-stool on which to rest after standing during his sermon. But once he began, he was the person I recalled seeing on television at previous crusades. He spoke powerfully, yet simply in message. I was spellbound hearing God's truth from such a humble messenger.

When he finished and gave the usual invitation to come forward to make a decision for Christ, I expected what I had seen at previous crusades. But no one moved.

At that time in my life, I was still living in the Prodigal pigpen of sin. I had volunteered to sing because I have always loved gospel music, the Gaither Vocal Band was performing, and it was Billy Graham! In retrospect, I know God orchestrated that night's events to prompt my return to an intimate, obedient walk with Him. When I noticed no one responding to Billy's invitation, my conscience pricked me. I was the Achan in the camp. God's spirit was restrained because of my sinful lifestyle. I was to blame for throttling spiritual revival at the Jacksonville Crusade!

Then I noticed what Billy did. That picture remains etched in my mind. He slowly leaned back on his chair-stool, placed his hands on the sides of the podium, bowed his head, and closed his eyes. It was a supernatural moment when the physical and spiritual realms are jointly visible to the human eye. Billy remained there, motionless, long, white hair gleaming like a lion's mane. There he sat, God's warrior statuesque, boldly grasping God's throne in prayer, and interceding for people he didn't know. Even me.

A spiritual shock wave then seemed to pulse through the stadium. People shot out of their seats like they were on fire and cascaded to the open space in front of the main platform. I could see tears streaming down faces as the crowd was pictured on the jumbotron television screens.

God's rainbow over Rotorua brought that cherished memory to life. It witnessed to His faithfulness between the storms and sunshine of life. His unconditional and universal love remains available for all. He paints His sky to remind us of His presence and invite us to His side.

The thunderstorm reminded me that the seasons of life befall us all — and death is everyone's inevitable storm. Billy Graham was prepared for his final storm and Heaven welcomed him the moment he breathed his last on earth.

Many people hunger and thirst for the peace, love, and assurance Billy Graham had and preached. Those who know Christ as personal Savior have already claimed the truth from God's Word: *For God so loved the world that He gave His only begotten Son, that whoever believe in Him should not perish but have everlasting life* (John 3:16).

From the rainbow over Rotorua comes this reminder: Don't let life simply pass by. Come to Jesus. Accept Him into your heart and life. Then, become an agent of change. Let God's light shine through you. Be a rainbow across someone's stormy skies.

Rest in Peace, Reverend Graham. I look forward to seeing you again one day. Until then, thank you for faithfully fulfilling your destiny and prompting me to return home.

4
In Everlasting Glory

Lola De Maci

When I heard that Billy Graham had gone to Heaven, a quiet peace fell over me. To have lived a long life of service to the Lord and his people by preaching the Gospel of the Lord Jesus Christ to millions has to be a life well lived.

I often wished that I could have met this remarkable man personally, but I didn't. However, I got to thinking . . . in my own way I did. Perhaps it's stretching it a bit, but I could claim to be part of Billy Graham's ministry by having written stories for the Moments books where all royalties go to Samaritan's Purse, an organization that helps those in need with the sole purpose of sharing God's love through his son, Jesus Christ. Billy Graham's son, Franklin Graham, is the president. Shamelessly, I brag to my friends that, in a roundabout way, I am related to the Billy Graham family. And proud of it.

Billy Graham has enriched my life tremendously. Yes, I cried as I watched his funeral on TV. I cried because he was such a beautiful man with a beautiful message. I am so grateful that he and I were here on this earth at the same time. His teachings encourage me and inspire me to be the best person I can be until one day I, too, will live in everlasting glory.

5

A Little Seed for a Little Girl

Jayme H. Mansfield

As the first dandelions emerge in the springtime grass, I'm assured plenty more will soon follow — appearing almost magically — until the grass is sprinkled with sunshine-yellow polka dots. Though a gardener's plight, these tenacious perennials thrive each summer when flower heads turn to downy seeds and disperse, eventually carried on the breeze to new resting places.

When I was a young child, a tiny seed found a new home in me — fertile soil that would eventually allow the seed to take root, grow, and blossom. The seed wasn't from a plant — destined to grow into a beautiful flower, a blooming bush, or even a sturdy tree. Instead, the seed was the Word of God, spoken by the Reverend Billy Graham at one of his many revivals, dispersed to thousands of people who had gathered to hear the Good News of Jesus Christ, carried on the "wind" of national television, settling into the homes of families across the country.

I didn't realize it at the time. I only knew the comfort of being snuggled beside my sweet-smelling mother on the family room couch. "It's your bedtime, honey," she'd say and then turn her attention again to the thick-haired preacher on the grainy television screen. I remember how he leaned into the pulpit, hands raised, and shouted words — not in anger, but with authority. I didn't understand much of what he said. But whatever it was, I knew it must have been important and that seemed to justify my refusal to go to bed (although I think my mother really didn't mind my disobedience at times like these).

My mother and I were mesmerized. Who was this man who spoke in large auditoriums, sports stadiums, and expansive parks that overflowed with mankind? Who were these quiet and captivated people — young and old, men and women, dark-skinned and light-skinned, some smiling, many weeping? And, why did my mother pull a tissue from the sleeve of her robe and dab at the corners of her eyes?

Over fifty years have passed since those special evenings, huddled with my mother on the couch and Billy Graham us through the television console. Still, the memory of his distinctive accent — calm like a lazy river, yet stirring as a waterfall, and rising and falling like the hills and valleys of the Blue Ridge Mountains — take me back to a time when the seed of God's word found fertile soil in the heart and soul of a little girl.

I now know the faces the camera panned across the screen were people — many lost, many found — all in need of a Savior . . . just like me. And, I understand why my mother cried. A mortal man, who spoke on behalf of God, inspired her. But more than anything, she was moved by the Spirit — tears of joy, tears of worry, and tears of gratitude and thankfulness to have her child by her side. Perhaps she knew (as mothers have a way of doing) that allowing me to listen to Billy Graham past bedtime invited a little seed to be tucked in my heart, stowed away until life insisted it grow . . . still growing . . . reaching for eternity.

6
THE STREET LIFE . . . OR MUSIC

Joseph S. Bonsall

The Billy Graham Crusade came to my hometown in 1961 for a month-long revival that started at the Philadelphia Civic Center and ended in Memorial Stadium (later renamed JFK Stadium and then torn down in 1992). Over 700,000 people came out to hear Rev. Graham that month, including more than 70,000 a night at Memorial.

I was one of those 70,000 for three straight nights near the end of the crusade. I was thirteen years old and in my formative, decision-making years, trying to decide if I wanted to listen to my mother — and the good folks at Calvary Church of the Brethren — or hang out on corners and become a street bum.

At that point, the wannabe hoodlums on the corner had the edge.

My mom and I walked three blocks to the church, where three school buses had lined up to take anyone who wanted to see Billy Graham. I'll admit I was excited. I had seen him on television. And, in 1961, if you saw someone in person who had been on television, and if you were thirteen . . . . Well, that was just huge.

The year before, my father had taken me to a *Thrill Show* at that very same Memorial Stadium in South Philly. It was acrobatics, motorcycles, and cool car tricks, and several television stars showed up. People like Sally Star and Carney C. Carney the clown. But the big star of the night was James Arness, aka USA Marshal Matt Dillon from the television show *Gunsmoke*. Little Joey freaked out seeing the marshal all decked out in his cowboy attire, complete with a holster and two fake (I assumed!) six guns.

So, I must admit, seeing Billy Graham was also kind of exciting to me. And others.

For three straight nights the huge crowd, the music, and the reverend himself as it turned out, would have a gigantic effect on me. Of course, I am almost seventy now, so much of it is a blur. Except that I remember him preaching directly to the city itself, a place that was facing a lot of racial division at the time. He told us that only Jesus and His amazing grace could heal the divides that separate us and that only the love that was manifested on the cross could save us from our sin. He also talked a lot about the promise of Heaven. It was amazing, and I was in total awe of this great man.

I wish I could say that I went forward as the choir and the masses sang "Just As I Am." But I did not. I sat by my precious mother and watched her pray, and my heart was filled with love, and a seed was planted that would lead to my accepting Jesus Christ as my personal Savior a few years later. That decision would lead me away from the street life and into a life of music, where I reside today as a forty-three-year member of the American music group The Oak Ridge Boys.

The Oak Ridge Boys for More Than 40 Years
Joe Bonsall, Duane Allen, William Lee Golden, and Richard Sterban
Photo courtesy Brandon Wood/IndieBling.

I had never thought much about Jesus until those nights at Memorial Stadium, but afterward He was all I thought about. I believe that God had a plan for my life. And I also believe He kept me from harm in those two years before I became a Christian.

Fast-forward more than thirty years to the White House in 1993. The Oak Ridge Boys and our wives had become friends with President George H. W. Bush (#41), and he had just lost the election to William Clinton, so he would not serve a second term. Early that January, President Bush invited us to sing in the East Room for the entire cabinet and congressional members. After we performed, we spent the night in the White House, which was all pretty surreal for a kid from Philly. But it was about to become even *more* surreal.

The next morning the president invited us to a special ceremony in the same room where we had sung the night before. He would be presenting former President Ronald Reagan with the Medal of Freedom. We took our seats among the small audience that had gathered, and lo and behold . . . seated to the left of my Mary and me was the Reverend Billy Graham.

He was as kind to us as you could imagine he would be. I shook his hand and fought back tears as he rose and led the room in a word of prayer. I wanted to tell him all about how much he meant to me . . . and about those nights in Philadelphia . . . and how much my mother loved him and . . . . But I did not. I just took in the moment and held my wife's hand. We were so privileged to be in that room at that time, and we would never forget it.

Now, the great man is at home with our Savior in the place that has been prepared for all such as him. My mom left in 2001, and I am sure she has found him by now and bent his ear pretty good.

The message of Billy Graham in Philadelphia in 1961 is the same message that is needed today. There is much division in our world and only Jesus Christ can provide the answer — and the love — needed to save us all. We must learn to stand upon the promises that Billy Graham preached about many years ago.

Where would the world be without the souls who were saved as a result of his ministry? Where would *I* be?

We have a song in country music called "Who's Gonna Fill Their Shoes?" No one can ever fill Billy Graham's shoes, but together we can all give it a try. And together we can SHINE THE LIGHT of JESUS CHRIST, for in HIM there is NO darkness at all.

7

A Godly Example for the Rebellious Heart

Diana Leagh Matthews

Growing up as a preacher's kid (PK) can be more challenging than rewarding at times. There is always the concern of how we will be perceived, what others will think, and how this will affect both the church and the ministry of our parents.

I did not realize until recently, how much I strived to be the perfect child and daughter when growing up. The last thing I wanted to do was to bring shame to Daddy or his ministry. However, that is exactly what I did upon reaching early adulthood. I lost my way, stumbled and made a lot of mistakes on my life's journey.

My rebellion intensified as my anger grew when God called Daddy home when I was twenty-five. I didn't understand why God took a man in not only his prime of life, but also his prime of ministry.

The faith I had been raised with never completely left me, but I did not have an intimate relationship with God for over a decade. I was full of rebellion and "I know best" thinking. I did not want to listen to the wise counsel of my parents, more-or-less listen to a sermon.

However, on multiple occasions while turning channels, I would stop to listen to the sermons of Billy Graham. His words reminded me that I was loved, and God still wanted me no matter how much I had sinned. These promises pierced my heart and God began to open my heart and mind to his promises of love and truth. As I began to remember these promises, I took a stand against the enemy. Eventually, I was so broken that I had nowhere to turn, except to fall on my knees before the Lord.

Billy Graham, the man and the father, shared openly that he was no stranger to the prodigal child. He admitted that as a teenager he'd had no interest in attending the camp meeting going on. But as days turned into weeks, his heart became curious and he attended the tent revival of Mordecai Ham. He began to attend night after night, until he surrendered his heart to Jesus. Graham's mother later said in an interview, "We saw a difference right away and knew God was working."

As we know, Billy Graham eventually became the great evangelist and "America's Preacher" that we saw in his crusades and through the media. However, as stressful as being a PK can be, can you imagine the stress that must have fallen on the five children of Billy Graham?

Ruth, his beloved wife, and his children endured not only his high profile, but his frequent absences. Looking back, it only seems natural that his children struggled.

His son, Franklin, titled his autobiography *Rebel with a Cause*. He shared openly about his own struggle with his faith and with his father's ministry. His rebellion led to his dad telling him that he and his mother sensed the struggle in Franklin's soul and he would have to make a choice. Making that statement could not have been easy, not knowing what his son would choose, but Billy Graham showed love, support and compassion to his wayward child.

At her father's funeral. Ruth shared the story of her rebellious past as an adult. Having ignored her parent's advice and realizing she'd made a monumental mistake, she was nervous about returning home. However, her father was waiting for her when she got out of her car. He wrapped his arms around her and said, "Welcome home." There was no shame, there was no blame, there was no condemnation — just unconditional love.

The Graham's youngest son, Ned, spoke of his struggle with drugs. He said is parents expressed concern and displeasure over his behavior but their love for him was always unconditional. "Eventually," he said, "their grace and love were just irresistible."

With his children, Billy Graham mirrored the father of the prodigal son as recorded in Luke 15:24 (NLT): *"This son of mine was dead and now has returned to life. He was lost but now is found."*

Oh, what love! Billy Graham's example was one that Mama followed during my own rebellious past. After three years of being separated with no contact, Mama greeted me with, "Let's put the past behind us and start from here." There were no questions and no condemnation. Instead, I was met with love, grace and compassion. I didn't deserve love and understanding, but genuine, Godly love sees beyond our faults and failures.

When I arrived home Mama and Grandmother met me with open arms and said, "Welcome Home." Mama recently told me that she was reminded of Billy Graham's humility that has served as a keen example and reminder of how to live life and treat others.

I am so grateful for a Christian mother who loved me and opened her arms to welcome her rebellious daughter home on more than one occasion. But, I also have Billy Graham to thank for this example. When a teenager, Mama rededicated her life to Christ at a Billy Graham crusade.

His example taught and inspired Mama to seek the Lord and ask His guidance to gently and lovingly welcome home a troubled daughter when she was broken and needed it most.

The ministry of Billy Graham does not stop with the hearts he has brought to God, but is passed down from generation to generation. Part of living for the Lord is to practice God's kind of love and forgiveness, even when it is not easy. After all, we often will never know the impact on the lives we touch and how those lives will one day touch others.

What a blessing for me, and millions around the world, to have learned from Billy Graham's example of living for Christ and exhibiting God's love to others in daily interactions.

8

NEVER THE SAME

Andrea Merrell

B illy Graham. A household name. A respected name. A name that will live on because of the legacy the man leaves behind. But it's more than just a name to me. When someone touches your life in a powerful way, your heart changes, and you're never the same.

When I was in junior high school, our town was buzzing because the young evangelist Billy Graham was coming to conduct a crusade. I had heard about this man and his ministry and wanted to see what the hype was all about. I remember walking into a large building filled to capacity with other curious and hungry souls. When the service began, everyone quieted as we waited in anticipation. Cliff Barrows led the crowd in worship, and then we were blessed by the musical talent and sweet spirit of George Beverly Shea.

But the icing on the cake, as they say, was listening to God's Word as it was delivered with a fiery passion by the man himself, Dr. Graham. Seeds were planted deeply in my heart that day, and I knew I would never be the same.

Fast-forward a few years. In the early days of my marriage, my husband and I were not living for the Lord even though both of us had professed Jesus as Savior. We were doing the best we could, but *something* was missing in our relationship and in our home. One night — sometime in my fourth year of marriage — while I was watching a Billy Graham crusade on TV God dealt with my heart. I began to weep. It became abundantly clear what was missing in my life, and I wanted it back.

Not too long after that, Dr. Graham conducted a crusade in Tampa, Florida, this time in a football stadium. Once again, every seat was filled. Excitement permeated the air. As the strains of contemporary Christian music filtered through the stadium, people stood to their feet, lifting voices, hearts, and hands to our great and mighty God. The venue, music, and methods were different, but the Word was the same. Its message was once again delivered with the passion that only one man could deliver. During the altar call, hundreds made their way from their seats to stand before the man who led them in a prayer of salvation. Their lives would never be the same.

As I look back over my life, I can see how the seeds that were planted in my heart as a young girl were watered and carefully tended by the One who engraved my name in the palm of His hand.

One day I — along with millions of others — will have the opportunity to thank Dr. Billy Graham for the part he played in my relationship with the Lord and my spiritual growth. Until that day, I hope my life will reflect even a small measure of the love and compassion he poured out to others during his lifetime.

9

BILLY AND DICKIE ARE GOOD BOYS

Nancy Johnson

I am now in my eighties. God has seen and answered the desires of my heart through the years. He has done things in my life that only He could do.

I worked as a counselor for the Billy Graham Crusades. It was my responsibility to go up to the front with an individual going forward to give their life to Christ. One time I went up with a lady who said the only reason she came forward was because she wanted to see what happened when people got up there!

I met African-American singer and actress Ethel Waters at one of the crusades when she was standing in the hallway. She was a very famous person at that time, best known for her song, "His Eye is on the Sparrow." She was a very nice lady.

One night when she was there, President Richard Nixon came to the crusade. He and Billy Graham were friends. A bunch of hippies had shown up to disrupt the services and protest one thing or another. They certainly hadn't come to hear about the Lord; they were just there to cause trouble, probably hoping they would draw attention to themselves and be seen and heard on television.

Ethel Waters shook her finger at them and spoke to them. "Billy and Dickie are good boys," she said. "Behave yourselves! What would your mother say to you if she was here and saw you?"

She sang that night . . . and I don't remember anybody misbehaving. Those who had come to protest their cause (probably because word got out that President Nixon was going to be there) heard the gospel instead.

I always thought a lot of Billy Graham. He refused to go to a meeting or minister in a place that was segregated. In fact, one time he went to a meeting and before the service started he found they had put a chain across an area for the black people to sit behind it. Mr. Graham told them to take it down, but they refused. So, Mr. Graham walked over and took the chain down himself. No one dared to put it back up.

Charles Fuller was a nationally known preacher at the same time Billy Graham was known internationally. In his meetings Mr. Fuller had a habit of saying, "God bless you on the right, and God bless you on the left."

I was at one of his meetings once where they had the chain up to keep us separated from the rest of the congregation.

Mr. Fuller said his usual, "God bless you on the right! God Bless you on the left!" Then he added, "And God bless you way back there!"

I called out, "He's talking about us!" A person had to try to keep a little humor about things during those times.

One year I sang in the choir at a crusade in Washington, D.C. I served as a counselor at a crusade in Kentucky. The last one I attended was in Knoxville, Tennessee.

Like Billy Graham, I wanted my life to count for something in God's work. I had a Bible story hour on the radio for many years and always loved to work with children.

Someone asked how many children I served over the years and how many I drove to Bible school. I have no idea really. I think it's safe to say it would be well over a thousand. I don't really know. Numbers didn't matter. I was doing what I was supposed to do. I never worried about a head count.

I do know that at least twenty-one men out of those children are now ministers of the Gospel of Christ. There may be more that I don't know about.

I have had people come up to me many times and tell me, "Miss Nancy, you made a difference in my life." Sometimes they say, "Going to Bible school with you kept me off the streets. It's hard to say how I would have turned out if you hadn't taken me to Bible school when I was young."

Teaching the Bible is the most important thing I've ever done in my life. It's what God called me to do. At my age, that's why I still do it! I could not have done anything without the Word of God and the power of prayer.

Billy Graham was a great servant of God. He obeyed the call that was on his life. We are responsible to answer the call that is on our own life.

10

Forbid Them Not...

Wendy Dellinger

While some people might think small children can't grasp the spiritual realities of salvation, I know differently. God came on the scene very early in my life with a strong and clear message to my child-heart — thanks to Billy Graham.

My parents were church-going, born-again Christians, and Sundays found my little sister and me dressed in our pretty dresses and headed off with them to church and Sunday school. I must have known about Jesus from my earliest days, but it wasn't until one night when I was five years old that I really met Him.

We sat in our living room watching a Billy Graham crusade on our black-and-white TV. He told how the Bible declares that we are all sinners, and using a vivid metaphor, he declared that sin gave us a black heart, but Jesus came and died for our sins so that we could have our hearts washed clean, forgiven and made new, with the gift of life in heaven forever with Him.

He was talking to *me*. I was struck to the core. Crawling up on the sofa next to my dad, I whispered, "Daddy, I have a black heart!"

He didn't laugh or make light of my earnest conviction. Gently he reviewed what we'd just heard Mr. Graham say about salvation and my need to deal with my now-understood sin issue. Jesus loved me. Jesus died for me.

"Would you like to ask Jesus into your heart right now?" he asked.

I nodded eagerly, and together we knelt down beside the sofa. He led me in the sinner's prayer, and to my five-year-old understanding, I got up *knowing* that I was a Christian, now with a clean, white heart.

No one can tell me that salvation can't be authentic in young children! Even though I recommitted my life to Christ years later with a more mature understanding, I knew without a shadow of a doubt from that moment by the sofa that I belonged to Jesus. I carried with me all my childhood years an inner knowing that He was in me and that I was saved.

Jesus welcomed the little children, saying to the disciples, *"Let the little children come to Me, and do not forbid them; for of such is the kingdom of heaven."* (Matthew 19:14) One day in heaven I hope to personally thank Brother Graham for his faithfulness to the Lord's call that could reach out and change the life of one small girl.

11
It's Polio!

Max Elliot Anderson

I remember hearing those words as if it were yesterday.

It was 1949. I'd just reached my third birthday. My oldest sister and one of my older brothers were already in the hospital. One of the neighborhood girls, Anita, had contracted the dread disease and died. We had a quarantine sign posted in the window that warned anyone coming near to stay away.

My mother came into the bedroom and asked, "Are you feeling okay?"

I nodded my head slightly, even though I couldn't lift it off the pillow. It hurt to turn my head from side to side. My throat hurt and there was a stiffness in some of my muscles. I was terrified. Still, I pretended nothing was wrong. "Uh huh," I groaned.

So, on a cold, grey, November morning, my mother bundled me up in my blanket. Then my father loaded me into the back seat of our car for a ten-mile trip to the doctor in Muskegon, Michigan.

During that trip, with snow piled up on both sides of the road, I kept whispering to myself, "Please don't let it be polio, please don't let it be polio, pleeease!" My parents hurried me into the doctor's office where the diagnosis was confirmed.

"It's polio."

I heard my parents talking with the doctor in the other room for the longest time. Though I couldn't make out the words, I knew something bad was about to happen to me. When they came back to where I waited, my father tried to act brave, but my mother had tears in her eyes. After all, they'd already received this crushing news twice before.

Many in the Baby Boom generation remember clearly the

polio epidemic in America when we were kids. We weren't allowed to visit our friends' houses and no one could come in and play with us. Families stopped going to church in some of the hardest hit regions in the USA, which included Massachusetts, New York, New Jersey, Michigan, Texas, Illinois, and Oklahoma. Many knew a friend, relative, or neighbor who had it. Even President Franklin D. Roosevelt suffered from polio, though he did his best to hide it from the public.

The cause of the disease wasn't known for sure, so parents feared the worst and didn't allow children to play with their friends, go swimming, or participate in activities around groups of other people. Because it seemed to thrive in the warm months, peaking in mid- to late-summer, polio was called The Summer Plague. At its peak in the 1940s and 1950s, Polio paralyzed or killed over half a million people worldwide every year.

In our home, this frightening journey began when my oldest sister started experiencing symptoms that included fever, headache, stiffness and sore throat. She was rushed to a hospital where the diagnosis came back quickly.

Polio!

I grew up in a family of seven children, so my parents rightly feared that one or more of the rest of us might also become infected. They were right. Not long after my sister was hospitalized, my older brother began complaining of stiffness. Polio had struck our family for the second time. Those of us who were left behind began wondering who would be next?

Most adults don't remember much about turning three years old. But memories of my third birthday could not be any clearer in my mind. I went straight to the hospital from the doctor's office.

Even now, I distinctly remember the smells in that place.

I also remember crowded conditions as we were quarantined in the polio ward. My brother and I were allowed to stay close together in crib-like metal beds. He was only four. He refused to speak, so I had to talk for both of us. At night, lights were always on. This, alone, made sleeping difficult, but there were also lots of noises, including other children crying in the night or calling out for their mothers.

Nurses were very nice to each of us, but staying in this strange place, away from family, wasn't easy. Our daily treatments included time in an iron lung to help with breathing, and baths in a metal tub of hot, swirling water.

Only our parents could visit us . . . just two days a week. On each visit, they brought my brother and me a brand new toy. That was significant because we didn't have much money. Every visit felt like Christmas.

Of the three of us in the hospital, I was the most severe. The doctor took my mother aside and spoke softly. "I'm sorry to tell you, but your son, Max, will never walk again."

Polio infected people from all ages and economic status. Many either died or became crippled for life. Years later I read that the area of Muskegon, Michigan, where we lived, was especially hard hit by this epidemic. Experts say it was carried in the water.

My father had worked with several ministries as a writer and in speaking engagements. He went to China with Bob Cook who would later found World Vision. He'd also been involved in ministry with Billy Graham. From September 25 through November 20, 1949 Mr. Graham and his team held a large crusade in Los Angeles, California. My birthday fell on November 3. My dad sent a telegram to Mr. Graham telling him that three of his children were hospitalized with this terrible, crippling disease. A return telegram informed my parents that Billy Graham had stopped his massive crusade meeting that day, and asked the entire audience to join him in prayer for the three Anderson children who were in desperate need just then.

Not long after that large prayer gathering, I, along with my brother and sister, were released from the hospital. The doctor, who had first diagnosed my condition as nearly hopeless, was particularly astonished by my dramatic recovery. My parents told him they knew exactly what had happened and how.

I especially remember that, because we'd been kept in isolation, we had to leave behind all those shiny trucks, cars, and other new toys our parents had brought us so faithfully. As a three-year-old, since I didn't fully understand the severity of my illness, I thought leaving the toys was the worst thing that had ever happened in my young life.

Polio had always been considered especially cruel because of the way it targeted children. At times it even seemed hostile. In the early 1950s, at the height of the baby boom, the numbers of polio epidemics' victims were rising even faster than the population. Mass infections continued until 1954 when Jonas Salk developed a vaccine, which stemmed the tide of this crippling killer.

In my adult life, it took many years before I could set foot in a hospital to visit a patient. That began to change after our children were born, though I still felt uncomfortable.

Then, a number of my professional video projects were for medical clients. I often dreaded entering hospitals to shoot footage. If I closed my eyes, in my mind, I was immediately transported back to those earlier hospital experiences as a three year old. Even now, when I have to go to my doctor's office for a checkup, my blood pressure goes up.

When our family is together for reunions or other family gatherings we still talk about those dark days.

Today, when I see someone wearing a leg brace, using crutches, or riding in a wheelchair, without fail I breathe a quiet prayer saying, "Thank you." Our healings have lasted over all these years. Not only am I able to walk normally, I have no lasting effects of any kind that would suggest polio had ever threatened my health or wellbeing. My brother and sister also remain completely symptom free from their illnesses to this day.

Much has been written about a condition called Post-Polio Syndrome (PPS). PPS affects approximately twenty-five to fifty percent of people who have previously contracted polio. The symptoms emerge fifteen to thirty years after recovery from the original attack, between ages thirty-five and sixty.

After years of prolonged stability, people who had been infected and recovered from polio start to experience new signs and symptoms including acute or increased muscle weakness, muscle pain, and fatigue in limbs that were originally affected. This can also be found in limbs that didn't seem to have been affected at the time of the initial polio illness. PPS is a very slowly progressing condition marked by periods of stability followed by new declines in the ability to carry out usual activities.

Could my sister, brother, or I experience symptoms of PPS? I suppose anything is possible; only God knows for sure. But I choose to believe the healing that came shortly after prayer during Billy Graham's crusade was not only dramatic, it was permanent. And it has been one of the anchoring points of my faith whenever doubts have crept in.

12

I *HAD* TO GO!

Lynn Mosher

In 1956, he was a young preacher, age thirty-seven. He preached twenty-six services over four weeks in Louisville, Kentucky.

My parents and grandparents held a large reception for him when he came to town and I vividly remember meeting Dr. Billy Graham. I remember shaking his hand and looking up as he towered over my tiny body.

I stood in awe. I don't know that any words came out of my mouth. As I looked into his crystal blue eyes, I thought I had just met Jesus!

I don't think my parents took me to the crusade. I have no recollection of attending. I was only ten years old. However, I do remember another crusade. One very important one that forever changed my life.

In the summer of 1957, Dr. Graham held his historic crusade in New York City. Between May 15 and September 1, he preached the gospel to more than two million people. After my eleventh birthday in July, my parents and I went to New York City to attend the crusade.

According to the Billy Graham Evangelistic Association, more than 56,000 people left their seats to go forward to pledge their lives to Christ during that time.

Being one of those thousands, I walked that concrete floor to the tune and words of "Just As I Am" and gave my heart to the Lord that night. I remember my mom trying to hold me back to wait until we got home to our church, but the Holy Spirit's tug was stronger than my mom's hand. I told her I *had* to go! I think she was more concerned about my safety in that large crowd of people.

That was now more than sixty-one years ago! That wonderful, eternal seed planted so many years ago has grown and flourished. And as a result of that spiritual planting, several other souls have been brought into the Kingdom and will enjoy heaven's bountiful feast.

I praise the Lord for the life of Dr. Billy Graham.

13

WORLDLY WEALTH, GODLY WEALTH

Gayle Fraser

On a snowy, freezing day in 1992, my husband and I bundled up for warmth. We were excited as we entered the grounds of the Great Kremlin Palace and visited the Armory Museum in Moscow.

Communism had opened its doors to the west. Members of our church made the trip over the great pond to participate in the Billy Graham Mission in one of the most secretive countries in the world. The trip was filled with mystery, intrigue, and contrasts. We considered being included in the Mission's effort a great privilege.

When ushered onto the grounds by our guide, the thought flashed through my mind, *this wealth is real.* We stepped inside the palace and museum where wealth abounded. Our guide briefed us on the ancient art history of Russia and the lavish treasures of Russia's Oriental and Occidental Art. Collections ranged from the twelfth through the seventeenth centuries. The royal splendor of the armory's gold and silver, crown jewels, manuscripts, coaches, and royal wardrobes were on display.

From that splendor we were transported by bus to the outskirts of Moscow where poverty was the norm. At the end of the block, we observed a large 2½-ton truck, draped with a canvas tarp, where men distributed bags of potatoes to people dressed in neutral colored wool coats, scarves, boots, hats, and mittens.

We passed storefront windows, in drab, gray, brown, and barren buildings. They displayed no colors that attracted attention and contained only a few items for sale.

There, we became part of the community as we blended with the businessmen, store owners and shoppers on the street, all headed to the only restaurant in town that served lunch. The restaurant was meager, with no inviting ambiance. Mix-n-match folding chairs sat at the metal frame tables with marble tops. In the USA, this would have been a throwback to the 1930's.

We took our place in line and followed whatever the person in front of us did. I was handed a clean, but tarnished bent fork and spoon. From across the service window, a large soup ladle poured a mixture of bouillon, potatoes and cabbage into our pie-tin plates. We received a metal cup filled with water. There were no crackers, biscuits or dessert, nor any salt and pepper or napkins.

From lunch we returned to our tour bus which took us to the Moscow Olympic Arena. Buses and cars were filling the spacious parking lot, without anyone to direct traffic. Civilians and military people mingled, laughed, and enjoyed each other's company. Our tour group walked to Arbot Street where we distributed information and encouraged attendance at the Billy Graham Mission during his three-day visit to Moscow.

As late afternoon approached, the crowds continued to grow. Everyone waited outside in the freezing cold for their turn to enter the stadium. The *Moscow Times* reported that the Mission broke all attendance records on all three nights. On Friday night the Mission attracted 42,000 people; Saturday night 43,500; and Sunday night 50,000 people. Additional people were outside in the freezing weather watching on a giant screen. A Graham spokesperson stated, "We believe that the crowds confirm there is a spiritual hunger here and a search for the meaning of life."

We stepped inside the frigid sports arena with no heat and hurried to claim a seat on cold concrete bleachers. We chose to sit in the back close to the doors, leaving the front seats for the Russians. I was thinking, *We came all the way around the world, to Russia, to attend a Billy Graham Crusade.* We were blessed.

I looked at the massive, angular concrete pillars that served as structural support for the sports facility. The floor, ceiling, bleachers and ramps were all concrete. No color, no painted trim, no advertising or promotions, no scoreboards — just concrete. Television cameras and audio-visual equipment with their cords were everywhere. Monitors and various other implements were set up on ten-foot, metal overhead stands. The facility was packed to capacity.

At the end of his sermon, Dr. Graham made his altar call. Personally witnessing tens of thousands of people who went forward — some literally running — like a tidal wave and approached the speaker platform was spiritually overwhelming. It started with a small wave and grew to massive proportions. First, fifty people rushed forward. That grew to one thousand people. The one thousand grew to ten thousand and finally, fifty thousand Russians — all ready and eager to accept God into their lives.

I witnessed the flow of bodies walking and running to Dr. Graham's invitation. After about thirty minutes of people leaving their seats, from on high to floor level, walking to the center of the arena, no one was left sitting in the bleachers. Then the Russian Army sang "The Battle Hymn of the Republic." They sang, "Mine eyes have seen the glory of the coming of the Lord," over and over, as we witnessed the miracle happening before us.

I experienced the worldly wealth and poverty of Russia all in the same day. It had been a stark and striking contrast. I experienced thousands of people becoming rich in faith, something that cannot be purchased with worldly wealth. I saw Scripture come alive before my eyes, as expressed in Matthew 5:3 (NLT), *"God blesses those who realize their need for him, for the Kingdom of Heaven is given to them."*

I'm so grateful for the ministry of Billy Graham, and the privilege of being part of that mission trip. How wonderful to know that no matter whether we're rich with splendor and gold, or standing in line for a bag of potatoes, we have access to the greatest kind of wealth, the love of Jesus and the riches of glory forever!

This wealth is real!

14
From Depressed to Blessed

Mary A. Hake

No one loves me. I doubt anyone ever will. I may as well kill myself.

Those thoughts often went through my mind during my senior year of high school. Classmates told me to my face, "No one really likes you." No guy ever asked me for a date.

Depression enveloped me with its ugly shroud, but I managed to keep my grades up. That was an area where I could achieve concrete results, and I liked to do my best. I also tried my best to be friendly, but didn't understand why my efforts seemed to fall flat.

I graduated in the upper ten percent, but couldn't find a job and couldn't afford to go to college. What did life hold for me?

Living at home with my parents after I turned eighteen made me feel like a kid. They still treated me like a child. I wanted independence and fun.

My locker partner from high school remained a friend, but we weren't super close. Her strong Christian family enthralled me. We often had spiritual discussions when I visited. One day she told me to be sure to watch the Billy Graham crusade on TV that night.

I had heard a little about this preacher, but had never seen a televised crusade. I told my dad I'd like to watch it. Dad controlled the living room TV and he planned to watch his program. He said, "I don't know why you want to watch that. But you can go use the old black-and-white TV in the family room.

So I did. I sat captivated from the first song. I had never heard anything like this. The words of the special music spoke to my heart. Then Dr. Graham preached a simple message. As I listened, my mind and heart opened to the truth. It was literally like a switch flipped to ON. I accepted the Lord Jesus Christ as my personal

Savior with tears streaming down my face.

Suddenly I felt loved! Truly loved! And I also felt love inside for others. I had to stop myself from telling everyone I saw, "I love you." I began treating my younger siblings better. My attitude toward my parents changed.

Actually, my entire life changed. I now hungered to read God's Word and sent for the free Bible the crusade broadcast offered. I also started to memorize Scripture.

The next month I found more love when I met the man who would soon become my husband. At first, I could hardly believe he loved me and found me beautiful. Perhaps he saw the love of the Lord shining through me.

That was more than forty-five years ago. I am so grateful to the Billy Graham ministry for holding crusades and televising them to reach the world for Christ. I was later blessed to attend two nights of a Portland crusade with my daughters and experience a crusade with Billy Graham in person. I have prayed for this ministry over the years, and I trust that his legacy of preaching the gospel will continue until Jesus returns.

15
Billy's Footsteps

Lowell Lytle

On February 21, 2018, I paused with the rest of the world to remember and appreciate the incredible ministry of Billy Graham, who "changed addresses" on that day as he said many times, moving from his earthly home to a new home in heaven. I had the privilege of meeting and working with Reverend Graham on several occasions in the 1950s, but that very first encounter, the moment I stood face to face with him and his lovely wife Ruth, was a moment of serendipity and absolute awe I shall never forget.

My older brother, Terry, and I both met the Lord early in life under the loving guidance of our mother. Throughout our childhood, our mother impressed upon us our urgent duty to reach the lost for Christ, and taught us how to share the gospel and use our God-given gifts at every opportunity for that same cause. Whenever we were not getting into mischief, we found many creative ways to do just that. It was a natural result, then, that Terry should enter the ministry, studying at Moody Bible Institute before being called to serve as pastor of a little church in Devil's Lake, Michigan. My decision to attend Moody came at age eighteen as I stood at a critical crossroad in my life. That same year Reverend Graham began Billy Graham Films, and the path to our mountaintop encounter with him was set. A portion of those incredible events, documented in my book *Diving into the Deep*, are recounted here:

> By 1950, drive-in theaters were wildly popular, allowing people to see a movie without having to dress up, find a baby-sitter, or even leave the comfort of their car. Terry

was one of a growing number of pastors who realized this concept might be a good way to spread the Gospel. If people would not go to church to hear the Gospel, they reasoned, perhaps they would come to a drive-in with their cars and listen to the message. Terry built a little platform at Devil's Lake in the middle of a cornfield for his first drive-in church. The building was sixteen feet wide, eight feet deep and eight feet tall, with room for storage and equipment underneath, and just enough room on the roof to put a piano. Loud speakers were attached to each side of the building. One evening my Moody music team drove in from Chicago to play at the drive-in church. The place was packed that night. "Wow!" I thought. "Maybe Terry is onto something."

The only problem seemed to be the location. It was right next to a swamp, and you can imagine how many bugs floated around in the night air. My father used to stand under the platform with a bug bomb, reaching up to spray the flood lights, where all the mosquitoes seemed to gather. That night, I was on the platform trying to play my trombone; with each breath, I would be siphoning mosquitoes through my teeth — no easy task. When it came time for the speaker, he handled the situation well . . . until he swallowed a bug. After hacking and coughing for about a minute, he said, "At least I was scriptural: 'He was a stranger, and I took him in.'"

Nine years later, Terry and I were working together in the midst of another screen building project, this time in St. Petersburg, Florida. We had not met Billy Graham, but as we expanded our ministry, we wanted to build a drive-in we could use to show Billy Graham films and other Christian productions.

Money was no object, because we didn't have any. I have always said there is a fine line between faith and insanity. We got hold of a real estate agent and said, "Show us ten acres of ground on Highway 19 between Clearwater and St. Petersburg."

He found just the spot and said, "It's only $40,000."

Well, in 1959 the average annual family income in the USA was about $5,600, but we said, "We'll take it." We didn't have even $40 to our name.

The more we stepped out in faith, the more we saw God's obvious work, and the greater our faith became. As faith grows, we can more easily recognize God's leading and become more emboldened, take on greater challenges. There is still fear, but God is not held back by fear.

Step by step, it was happening. That September, Terry and I followed up on a contact with a Florida woman who had the capacity to provide considerable support. Mrs. Cannon was heir to a retail soft goods dynasty. She wintered on St. Petersburg Beach, but lived in North Carolina most of the year. We couldn't wait until winter to speak with her, so we got in Terry's station wagon and drove all night to North Carolina.

On our way, we went through a little town called Montreat. Terry said, "I believe Billy Graham lives here. It sure would be nice to see his house."

We stopped and asked a lady where he lived. "Are you ministers?" she asked.

Terry answered, "Yes."

She pointed to a road that led up a mountain. "Go halfway up there," she said, "and you will see his house."

We started up the mountain on a one-lane dirt road. After about two minutes I questioned, "What are we doing? We have no business doing this." First, we had slept all night in our clothes, and our car smelled like an old boxing gym; and second, we were about to invade Billy Graham's privacy. We looked for a place to turn around, but there was none. I said to Terry, "When we get to his house, we'll turn around and go back."

When we arrived, we saw Ruth Graham standing outside trimming her hedges, and she saw us, too. We stopped, got out of the car, and apologized. "We just wanted to see where he lived," I said, and quickly tried to explain that we had a Christian drive-in theater in Michigan and had many times seen her husband's face on our large screen. "We'll just turn around and go back."

"No," she said. "He just got back from Africa last night and would love to see you." She turned and went into the house.

A few minutes later Billy Graham appeared. He was sporting a red shirt and a beautiful suntan, and looked bigger than life. As he started walking toward us, I felt a stupid grin on my face and blurted out, "There he is!" Then I thought, "Oh, no!" But I couldn't take it back. When he came up to us, we shook his hand. I said, "My name is Lowell Lytle."

He then looked at Terry, but Terry was in shock. He tried to say his name twice, but each time it came out backwards, so he stopped trying. We briefly told Billy what we had been doing and what our plans were for the future. He thought it was a great idea and he encouraged us. He ended our meeting by praying for us. We never did see Mrs. Cannon.

Terry Lytle, Billy Graham, Lowell Lytle

God used that brief encounter to embolden and encourage us, and later we would put that boldness to good use, leading to yet another fantastic and serendipitous encounter with Dr. Graham, the details of which you may enjoy reading in *Diving into the Deep*.

December 1965 we finally finished building the Florida drive-in and were open for business, presenting Billy Graham's *The Restless Ones* for our first showing. One of the most modern drive-in theaters in the country was brought into being through two brothers with a passion and vision for the ministry and the help of countless others obedient to God's call to support us in every way a ministry can be supported, including the prayers, encouragement, participation, and blessings of Billy Graham.

Though each drive-in eventually became obsolete, the ministry continues to this day in hard-to-reach countries, sharing the gospel through movies and talks given from a mobile pop-up stage and screen.

Over the years, watching Billy Graham's films and seeing the boldness with which he presented the gospel message made a huge impact on my life.

Some of the last words that Christ spoke to his followers were, "Go into all the world and preach the gospel to every creature." For those of us who are believers, that is not just a suggestion. We are Christ's ambassadors, though often we fail in that responsibility.

In fact, I have been told that ninety-seven percent of all Christians have never led a soul to Christ. If we were to ask that same ninety-seven percent if they could quote five Scripture verse besides "Jesus wept" and John 3:16, many could not do it. If you are among the ninety-seven percent, you may think you are not "good enough" to lead another person to Christ, not capable, or that you should not offend anyone with the gospel. That is a lie you should not believe. Scripture tells us the Holy Spirit will show us what to say when God gives us the opportunity. We should not hesitate to speak up.

Billy Graham's ministry continues through you and me. He followed in the Lord's footsteps. Let us do the same, obey our Lord's command, and be bold ambassadors for Jesus Christ.

16

CERTAINTY

Diane H. Pitts

The fumes of the bus seeped through the open window and mixed with the chatter of teenagers returning from a Saturday night revival in 1971. The warmth from the simple gospel songs could not stem the icy river in my heart or the isolation I felt.

"You never do enough. All those people will die and go to hell because of you." The inner voices of condemnation brought me to my knees, crushing any assurance of my standing with God.

I showed up at Sunday school the next morning. *On Time.* Check, I thought. Might as well mark the other boxes on the offering envelope.

Brought Bible. Check.
Made contacts. Check.
Included Offering. Check.
Brought Visitor. Not checked. *Uh, oh. Maybe I can bring my neighbor next week.* A cloud of self-doubt swept across my spirit. I dropped the envelope in the offering plate, but no wave of approval followed.

We sang songs, met visitors, and heard announcements — the normal routine before splitting to individual classes. The final announcement caught my attention.

"We need counsellors for the Billy Graham film, but it requires a commitment of six weeks. Volunteers meet with the lead counsellor every Sunday afternoon at First Presbyterian Church." The superintendent smiled and scanned the room. "And there *is* homework."

I was the first one to sign up. *Surely God would be pleased with a sacrifice of time, wouldn't He?*

For six weeks I looked up verses in the lessons provided by the Billy Graham Association. I gravitated to the verses assuring people salvation was based on a sacrifice. But it wasn't a human sacrifice of time or effort. God sent His Son to be the sacrifice for anyone who believed. This simple knowledge contradicted everything I felt.

Jesus.

Entry into heaven. Check.

Assurance of God's acceptance forever. Check.

Jesus' righteous life in exchange for my sin. Check.

I finished the course and showed up for the film as a counsellor. Scared, but willing.

Was the icy river in my heart thawed? The truth of Scripture penetrated my emotional glacier and began a process which is still continuing.

To undo wrong thinking.

To let God provide what I never could.

To bring me peace of mind and soul.

Thank you, Mr. Graham for keeping it simple and true. I will see you again one day. I'm certain.

17
THE LAST TWO DOLLARS

Carlene Shuler Brown

I looked through the window of the neighborhood drug store and saw several of my friends sitting at the soda fountain. My best friend, Jeannie, was among them, sipping on a cherry coke. I walked in and she motioned to the empty stool next to her that she was saving for me.

"Hi Jeannie, what are y'all talking about?"

"We're talking about our trip to Ridgecrest next month," she answered. "Everybody's going."

I looked down at the floor, trying to hide the tears welling up in my eyes. "I may not be able to go."

Jeannie's eyes widened and her mouth gaped open as she shouted. "What? You have to go."

* * *

It was the summer of 1957, and I was twelve years old. On Sunday, my Sunday school teacher announced that the church was planning a weeklong trip the next month to Ridgecrest Baptist Assembly in North Carolina for the young people. She said it was a great opportunity because Billy Graham would be there preaching every night. I had heard a lot about him and had seen him on TV.

"That would be so much fun," I whispered to my friend sitting next to me. "And I'd love to see Billy Graham in person."

My heart dropped when she told us that it was going to cost twenty-five dollars for each person to cover the expenses for the trip. I knew my father didn't make a lot of money as a Sergeant in the Air Force, and twenty-five dollars was a lot of money. I was so afraid he'd tell me I couldn't go.

I didn't say anything on the ride home from church, but went straight to my room to change clothes before we gathered in the kitchen for Sunday dinner. Later, as I set the table, I tried to think of what I could say to convince them to let me go on the trip. I ate in silence for most of the meal, afraid to bring up the subject.

When we were about finished, Mama spoke up. "Is something bothering you?" she asked. "You've been so quiet all through dinner."

I took a deep breath and held it for a second or two. Then it all came tumbling out in a torrent of words.

"My Sunday school teacher told us about a weeklong trip to Ridgecrest next month and Billy Graham is going to be there and it costs twenty-five dollars and I want to go." There! It was out. But as I watched Mama and Daddy look at each other, I knew what he was going to say.

"Honey, I know you want to go," he said. "And we would love for you to go too. But with a baby coming, and new school clothes to buy for you and your brother, I'm afraid I don't have the extra money to give you."

"But Daddy, I just have to go. All my friends will be there."

"Honey, I'm sorry. If you can raise the money yourself, you can go. But we just don't have it."

I was crushed. I sat there, my mind spinning, trying to figure out how I could get the money. My parents gave me two dollars a month allowance, and sometimes I would babysit for my neighbors and get paid thirty-five cents an hour.

"It's impossible," I cried. "How could I ever get that much money in time?"

I pushed away from the table and ran to my room, slamming the door behind me as tears streamed down my face. I threw myself on my bed and cried, trying to think of what I could do. I really wanted to go on that trip.

After a while, I went into the living room, and sat down next to my mother on the couch, watching her crochet. Finally, I spoke. "Mama, I want to go to Ridgecrest so bad, but it's impossible for me to make that much money. I just can't think of anything I could do. With my allowance and babysitting, I might get a few dollars and that's all."

Mama pushed aside the baby blanket she was making. She took my hand in hers and looked deep into my eyes as she spoke. "Honey, God loves you," she said. "And He wants the best for you. Pray, and ask God to help you. If it's His will for you to go, He'll provide the money."

"But it would take a miracle to get that much money in time by myself," I cried.

"God still performs miracles," she said. "It happens more than a lot of people realize. Just pray, and then trust in God to provide."

I walked back to my room and sat on the bed, thinking about what she had said. How does God provide, I wondered. Would the money miraculously appear somewhere? Would it just float down from Heaven? I didn't know all that much about faith yet, and I couldn't figure out how it was supposed to happen. But I knew my mother was right.

I had prayed before, but it was usually just words like thanking God for things, or asking him to bless my parents, and the food, or something like that. I had never prayed for a miracle and really wasn't sure how. But I said, "God, you know how much I want to go on this trip. Please help me get the money to pay for it."

* * *

Everyone in the drug store stopped what they were doing and turned to look at us. Embarrassed, Jeannie turned back to me and lowered her voice to a whisper as she asked, "Are you saying you might not get to go?"

"Maybe," I said.

"But why?" she asked.

"Daddy said that he doesn't have the extra money to give me, so if I want to go, I have to raise the money myself."

Jeannie slurped the last of her cherry coke through the straw. She stared at me for a second, then laughed and wrinkled her nose.

"You can't be serious. You can't raise that much money yourself. What could you do?"

"I don't know. There aren't that many babysitting jobs, and there's nothing else I can think of to do." I looked at her and took a deep breath. "But I've just got to find a way."

We talked a bit more about the trip as I enjoyed what I figured would be my last coke float for a while. If I were to have a chance of going to Ridgecrest, I had to save all of my money.

As we rose to leave, the pharmacist called out for me to come over to see him. I told Jeannie goodbye and walked over to his counter.

He smiled. Then he said, "I couldn't help overhearing your conversation, and I know how you can make some money." I looked at him as if he'd just turned into my fairy godmother.

My eyes got big as saucers. "Really . . . I mean, how?"

He laid a pad of certificates in front of me and explained they were for family portraits from one of the local photographers. "If you sell these certificates, you'll get one dollar for every one you sell."

I was stunned! I could hardly believe what I was hearing. My prayer was answered. God was providing a way for me to make some money.

Still in a daze, I thanked him as he handed me the certificates. "You don't know how much this means to me," I said.

"I think I do," he said with a wink and a smile. "You just get busy selling those, and when you get back from Ridgecrest, you can tell me all about it."

I ran out the door and didn't stop until I got home. I burst in the front door, about to explode with excitement, as I called out, "Mama, you'll never believe this."

When I calmed down a little and caught my breath, I finally got it all out. Mama gave me a big hug and said, "See, I told you God would provide. But you're going to have to work hard to sell all those certificates."

"Oh, I will, Mama. I really will. I'm going out right now."

Starting that afternoon, I went from door to door in my

neighborhood every day, trying to sell the certificates. It wasn't easy. Even though the families only had to pay me one dollar for the certificate, they had to pay the photographer twelve more when they went to get their family picture taken. Some days it was hard, and I didn't sell any certificates. But I kept on going up one side and down the other side of the streets in the neighborhood. It took almost the whole month, but I just wouldn't stop until I sold them all.

I saved my allowance and some money I earned from babysitting. But I still didn't have all the money I needed, and I didn't know how else I could get more. I had been praying every night, thanking God, but with time running out, I prayed even harder.

Late in the afternoon, the day before we had to turn in our money for the trip, I was still two dollars short. Jeannie and I had been together all afternoon and were discussing my problem as we walked barefoot down the sandy dirt road to her house.

"How are you going to get the last two dollars?" she asked.

"I don't know," I sighed. "It's impossible. Here it is, the last day, and I have no way to make any more money. Daddy has already given me my allowance early for next month, so he probably won't give me any more."

As Jeannie and I walked along in silence, I looked down at the road, kicking at the sand with my bare feet. Were all my prayers and hard work were for nothing? I had tried so hard to raise the money so I could go on this trip and see Billy Graham.

Suddenly, I noticed something at the edge of the road. I stopped and looked for a second, then walked over and picked up a wad of crumpled paper. As I started unfolding it, my eyes grew wide with astonishment. It was two, one-dollar bills.

I just stood there, staring at the money. I was almost afraid to breathe for fear that it would disappear. When it didn›t, I became excited and started jumping up and down. I thought my heart would burst with joy.

"Look Jeannie," I cried. "It's the last two dollars. God did provide. He provided it all."

Jeannie squealed and jumped up and down with me.

As thankfulness filled my heart, I looked up into the clear blue sky, almost expecting to see God smiling down at me and saying, "You're welcome."

My own smile grew wider as I said to myself, *Maybe, sometimes it does just float down from heaven!*

* * *

Well, I did go to Ridgecrest. And it was everything I thought it would be. Billy Graham preached every night and he was wonderful. We had such a good time with our friends too.

The last night, a friend and I snuck out of preaching a little early and went around the back, hoping to see Billy Graham. He hadn't come out yet but his driver was there and we started talking to him, asking him questions about Billy Graham. We asked if Mr. Graham would sign our Bibles. He said that he didn't normally do that, but he would ask. He took our Bibles inside.

We patiently waited by his car, nervously giggling about Billy Graham signing our Bibles. I wondered how many twelve-year-old girls had asked him that.

Soon, Billy Graham walked out, nodded to us and got in the car. The driver discretely gave us our Bibles and they drove off.

When we looked at our Bible, it was inscribed, "God Bless You, Billy Graham."

18

ENGLISH 101: PASS OR FAIL?

By Lydia E. Harris

As a college freshman, I got a rude awakening to find that class sizes often exceeded my entire high school senior class. Then, getting a D– on my first English paper made me wonder whether I would pass or fail.

I needed a course correction — fast. The next assignment was to write a paper to convince others. First, I needed to convince myself that I could write. So I chose a topic I felt passionate about: Billy Graham. I had heard him speak and admired his courage and faith.

With plenty of research and prayer, I completed my convincing argument and turned it in.

When it was time to retrieve my paper, I had gone from a D– to an A+! One day I'd like to thank Billy Graham for his help.

But Billy Graham's influence in my life didn't end with college. After my husband and I married, we attended the local Billy Graham crusade meetings and sang in the crusade choir.

Years later, in another crusade, our college-aged son joined us in the choir. I felt thrilled to be part of Billy Graham's evangelistic outreach and to witness hundreds of people stream forward as we sang "Just As I Am."

I later applied my college courses and became a writer. I remember getting the *Decision* magazine from the mailbox. I held it close to my heart and thought, *Anyone who writes for Billy Graham's magazine has really arrived as a writer.* But as quickly as that thought came, God's voice whispered, "Anyone who obeys Me on a daily basis has really arrived. I don't need everyone to write for *Decision.*"

Throughout my life, Billy Graham has been a steadfast example of faithfulness, godliness, and obedience. Although I never met him face-to-face, I admired his humility and holiness. He went to glory just a few days after my sister did, so I imagine she was part of a cheering crowd that welcomed him home.

Thank you, Billy Graham, for serving the Lord and impacting me throughout my lifetime. You didn't need an earthly grade to pass the class. You've received one far greater.

Well done, good and faithful servant.

Matthew 25:23 NLT

19

A Hero of Faith

Amanda Hughes

The example for Christ that Billy Graham displayed through the words he preached and the life he lived, impact me today and will always.

My parents had the privilege of hearing him speak in person; however, while I was growing up, I listened to the specials that aired on television. I recall the beautiful hymns George Beverly Shea sang about God's grace and salvation, and the gospel message Pastor Graham preached. Even when the same program broadcast again and again, it never got old to me.

I knew his ministry was about helping people come to trust Jesus as savior, not about himself. At the same time, it was important that I recognized there were people like Pastor Graham in the world who consistently shared the gospel. He was a prominent figure, growing ever large in the public eye, yet he remained faithful to God, his family, and calling.

It was clear that he wasn't trying to prove anything for himself, but wanted people to learn of God's gift of salvation through Christ's work on the cross. He was genuine, able to speak as someone who cared more what God had to say to than what Billy Graham had to say.

I had trusted Jesus as my savior before I knew of Billy Graham or listened to him preach the gospel. However, I was grateful to know who he was, and especially learn what he stood for. He served as a hero of faith to me.

Watching his life, over the years of my youth, taught me to stand strong even when circumstances seemed impossible. I learned from him that if I trusted God, and if he had a plan to do something in my life, he was going to do it in his way and time. When I heard Pastor Graham speak, I went away encouraged to continue seeking God's will for whatever he was calling me to. Everything would work out in God's timing, with God's ability to follow through, because of His own faithfulness that never fails. This stayed with me through the years and is something I remember about Pastor Graham's preaching. That gave me a deeper faith of understanding who God is, and should be in my life.

I grew more in love with Jesus because I would hear how much Jesus loved me first, with the kind of love that would never end. I never grew bored hearing the gospel message. The truth about God's love for each of his human creations, and that he had a purpose for my life came across in such a way it was evident every person who heard any sermon preached by Pastor Graham was prayed for by him and his ministry team.

Pastor Graham was a man America and the whole world needed, and God used mightily. The good news about the Good News he shared is God will continue to use the ministry of Billy Graham in my life, a ministry that will also reach countless others throughout the generations to come.

20

WHAT HE LOOKED LIKE

Judith Victoria Hensley

Billy Graham spent his life teaching others about the love of God through Jesus Christ. The lives impacted by one man answering the call to carry the gospel are innumerable. An ordinary man from a simple background became globally acknowledged and synonymous as a man of God with a message of love, redemption, and hope.

I had first heard of Billy Graham and the tent revival movement when I was a child. Through decades of life, I watched news coverage of those packed tent meetings turn into stadium events where thousands of people poured in to hear the Word of God from the lips of this southern gentleman. His calling and convictions always poured through with dignity and determination. He was about the Father's business.

In college I trained to be a counselor for one of the Billy Graham Crusades. I was amazed at the number of people who stood up and went forward at the invitation. This man's words from the Bible caused people to make life-altering decisions. He spoke simply and extended truth and hope in something bigger than himself.

I heard a message once about a man who dreamed he died and went to heaven. In the dream he apologized to God for not being "a Billy Graham." God's response was that He had not called that individual to be Billy Graham. He had created that person with his own unique purpose and destiny and he wasn't expected to measure up to the purpose God had placed in Billy Graham's life.

I recently paid a visit to the Billy Graham Library in Charlotte, North Carolina. As we walked through the family home and grounds, I was impressed with the simplicity of the early life of this world known evangelist. There was nothing in that part of his life that would have predicted the outcome.

As we walked through the halls of the library reviewing different events in the beloved evangelist's life, I was still amazed at all one man had accomplished for the kingdom of God. The Holy Spirit spoke to my heart very clearly. "This is what My authority looks like on a man's life."

Billy Graham knew who he was, and he knew who God was. He understood that what he accomplished for the kingdom of God was because God had appointed him to the task and he was compelled to fulfill that great commission.

In one room, as we watched videos of Billy Graham preaching the gospel, invited by leaders who had previously forbidden the gospel in their nations, the Holy Spirit spoke to me again. "This is what my favor looks like on an individual's life."

God opened doors for Billy Graham that no man could open. As God's servant, he had been taken on a journey to parts of the world that had been sealed off from the Good News of the gospel. Because he said, "Yes!" when God called him to go and had been an obedient servant, God took him on the most incredible journey that perhaps any human being has known.

As I watched a recording of Billy's last interview with Greta Van Susteren, the Holy Spirit spoke to me again. "This is what humility looks like."

Through all the review of his life in the halls of the Billy Graham library, there was never a time that he tried to proclaim his own importance or elevate his own ministry. Consistently, he gave God credit for all that had been accomplished through his life. In every sermon, every article, and every interview, Billy Graham lifted up the name of Jesus Christ. His personal power and passion were rooted and grounded in the Word of God. He never backed down from anyone or their critical questions. He was not afraid to answer because his answers were found in the Bible.

The message with which he began his incredible journey and the message with which he ended it were the same: We are all sinners in need of a Savior. Every person has a hole inside that only relationship with God can fill. Because God loved us so much, He sent his only begotten son so that whoever believes in Him and accepts His love and sacrifice does not have to perish, but can have everlasting life.

21

Linking Generations with a Chain of Faith

Shirley Brosius

When I was a child, my family attended church and Sunday school — without fail. We prayed at meals and at bedtime — without fail. My parents read Bible stories to me. They were honest, hard-working people, wonderful Christian role models who shared a legacy of faith with their children.

In my early teens, I attended Confirmation classes at my church and filled in the blanks in my denominational Catechism book. The pastor explained the Ten Commandments, the Apostles Creed and other basics of the faith, and I wrote answers to "Questions to be Answered by Catechumens."

The day of Confirmation, I solemnly knelt to take my first communion and took seriously my profession of faith in Christ. I believed. Almost.

You see, we lived on a farm, and as I looked at evening skies, I often wondered what it would be like if Jesus suddenly broke through the clouds. But there was the rub. I just wasn't quite sure if Jesus was who everyone said He was. Why would an All-Powerful God, Ruler of the Universe, let His Son be tortured to death? It didn't make sense.

Although I asked one pastor, then another, their answers did not satisfy me.

As a business education teacher, I spent evenings correcting papers. As I worked I watched television and, from time to time, a Billy Graham crusade. Billy explained that God was perfect and holy and no imperfection could ever come into His presence. Billy said God required a perfect sacrifice to pay the penalty for our wrongs, our sins.

He explained that Old Testament offerings and sacrifices just "covered" the sins of the people; they did not erase them for good. That was why God sent His Son, Jesus, to serve as a perfect sacrifice. That was why Jesus had to die.

I had no trouble understanding that I had done things that were wrong, and as I read my Bible, the verses finally made sense. I also read books by Christian authors, such as Catherine Marshall, who echoed Billy Graham's explanation.

At Christmastime the year I turned thirty, I sat in the twinkling lights of my Christmas tree and told God I was through analyzing and questioning whether Jesus was His Son. I finally understood I could never lead a perfect life, acceptable to God, on my own. I needed a Savior. And whether what I had professed at Confirmation was enough or not, I invited Jesus into my heart.

Billy Graham invited viewers to send him their names and addresses to indicate they had made a decision for Christ, so I did. In response, I received a small red booklet that led me through scriptures assuring me of my salvation. In the back were perforated cards with Bible verses to tear out and memorize. I completed the booklet. Little did I realize I was forging a link in a chain of faith that would reach far beyond my home.

Because my Savior had given His life for me, I wanted to give something back to Him, so I volunteered to teach an after-school Bible club. Each Wednesday afternoon more than twenty neighborhood kids joined my two sons in our living room to drink juice, eat cookies and hear Bible stories. They memorized verses, and as Billy Graham had led me to the Lord, so I led several of them to the Lord.

In time, I earned a master's degree in Christian education and served for ten years as a director of Christian education. Then the Lord opened doors to a writing career, and I published a devotional book for women.

In 1998, Kim and Janine, young enough to be my daughters, asked me to be their mentor. We met weekly at 5:30 A.M., while their husbands were home with their children, to discuss Christian books.

Wanting to serve as well as study together, we visited shut-ins and held teas to encourage women facing challenges. Then we developed a women's retreat for Kim's church, and we enjoyed ministering to ten women, ranging in age from a high schooler to two octogenarians.

Dubbing ourselves "Friends of the Heart," we invited several women's ministry leaders to a tea and offered to lead retreats for their churches. We also developed a website. That first year we led just one retreat, but now, twelve years later, we lead about twenty events a year and have spoken to at least 10,000 women in seven states.

My stash of scripture has grown since I memorized those perforated cards from Billy Graham's booklet. At our retreats, I present lengthy passages from memory — the Book of Ruth, the Book of Philippians, the first four chapters of John's Gospel. And, of course, we present Jesus as our Lord and Savior. Besides speaking, Kim, Janine and I wrote a devotional book together so that women have readings to encourage them after inspirational events.

One of my sons is a pastor, and the other son's wife is a director of children's ministries. My grandchildren have taken mission trips.

What a privilege to share in Billy Graham's legacy of bringing people to Christ — through children's ministries, through mentoring, through work as a director of Christian education and now through my work as a writer and speaker. I trust that my teaching and testimony equips others to serve as links in the chain of faith to reach future generations.

22

BILLY GRAHAM WAS ALL IN

Diana Leagh Matthews

Rain beat down on us that spring evening in 1987, but we did not care. We opened our umbrellas and held them high. Nothing would deter us from having the opportunity to sit in the choir bleachers at Williams Brice Stadium for those eight evenings Billy Graham was holding his crusades.

We arrived early each evening, and Cliff Barrows led us in rehearsing the specials. The service was filled with guest speakers and vocalists, including Miss South Carolina 1986, Dawn Smith, followed by George Beverly Shea with his deep, rich, baritone voice. After Bev Shea finished singing, Billy Graham stepped to the podium and preached a message of God's love and redemption.

Before we reached the stadium that spring evening, my soon-to-be teenager self was already familiar with Rev. Billy Graham. I had read some of his books and heard him preach on TV many times. Whenever his crusades aired, we tuned in.

During the crusade, I was moved by the music and riveted by the message of Jesus' love that was shared from the podium. Tears poured down my cheeks as thousands came forward to give their lives to Christ.

Even in the years following the crusade, especially while I had a spirit of rebellion, struggling to find myself, and struggling with my faith and calling, I would still stop to listen any time I came across a Billy Graham crusade on TV. Those nuggets of truth stayed with me and eventually I re-surrendered my heart, and life to Jesus.

On Wednesday, February 21st, 2018, Billy Graham made his final journey. He left his earthly body for his heavenly home. Once there he met our Lord and Savior, whom he dedicated his life to preaching and sharing the message of His [Jesus'] love. Billy was also reunited with his beloved wife, Ruth, and those on his ministry team, including his long-time musical counterpoints and ministry partners, Cliff Barrows and George Beverly Shea.

Time and again in interviews we hear the Graham family say, "We will miss him, but we're rejoicing because he is now home."

Billy Graham lived out his calling and his faith. In interview after interview we hear the following things said about him:

- Shared the message that God loves us
- The same person in private as in public
- Always humble
- Pointed toward the cross and away from himself
- Man of robust integrity
- Passion for his message
- United people
- Bridge Builder between people
- Encourager of others
- Mentor to young people
- Spoke and lived a life of honesty and truth
- Lived his life for the Lord
- Admitted when he was wrong
- Walked intimately with the Lord
- Kind and gracious
- Faithful to his calling
- Forgiving
- Man of devout faith
- Showed interest for those he spoke with
- Unconditional love
- Gave ALL of the glory to God

Billy Graham strived to live for his Lord and to show God's love to others. He lived his life verse, which his son Franklin stated was posted throughout the house. *God forbid that I should boast except in the cross of our Lord Jesus Christ, by whom the world has been crucified to me, and I to the world.* Galatians 6:14

As he stood before the Lord in heaven, there is no doubt that God said, "Well done good and faithful servant."

Christians can strive to emulate the faith and integrity of Billy Graham. Regardless of the calling God has placed on our lives, Billy Graham serves as a reminder to me, that we should live it out with all our heart and soul, in not just our words but also our actions.

I heard these words in a movie I recently saw: "Are you all in or all out?"

Billy Graham was definitely all in, for his Savior.

With a Prayer and a Smile

John Jaruczyk as told to Barb Suiter

John Jaruczyk, a shy twelve year old watched for a chance to introduce his small brother, Andre, to Billy Graham. His family had been at the 1983 crusade in Orlando, Florida each evening. His mother, Nina, and two sisters sang in the choir. Russell, his father was a counselor. John was with Andre every service.

A friend had sat with the two boys the previous nights, but on Saturday, the last night, Nina needed to find someone else, or a place where the boys would be safe.

A security guard near one of the gate entrances at the Citrus Bowl Stadium said to Nina, "Leave the boys right here by me. They will be out of the sun and away from heavy foot traffic. I will keep my eye on him and his brother." So Nina left Andre, supported by a chest brace, in his special stroller.

Having been twenty-four weeks premature, weighing only 1.1 pounds, Andre had lived against all odds and medical opinions. John was proud of his little brother, now eight and weighing thirteen pounds.

John took Andre out of the stroller and laid him on a blanket about midway through the service. When the crusade ended, Dr. Graham walked near John and Andre.

John immediately approached Dr. Graham and said, "I want you to meet my brother. When he grows up, he will be a preacher just like you." He shook the outstretched hand of Billy Graham.

"I would like to meet your brother," Billy said and smiled as John led him to the blanket. Billy Graham bent down and picked up the small child; then he knelt on one knee and prayed.

John helped Andre stand, and he placed one arm around Dr.

Graham's neck as his long-time friend, photographer Russ Busby, snapped a photo. Then, Dr. Graham stood and thanked John for introducing him to his little brother.

As Dr. Graham left the stadium, he shared the incident with one of the local pastors who knew the Jaruczyk family. "Now, I have no need to worry," Billy said. "God has my substitute."

Can you imagine the smile on his face as he said that?

Today, though blind and confined in many ways, Andre responds magically to music. It is life to him. Often as worship music is sung and played in church, Andre "preaches" to all as he bursts into appropriate spontaneous applause with guarded shouts of praise.

John always believed that the multiple, subsequent surgeries Andre required were successful due to that special prayer of Billy Graham's that evening. Thirty-five years later, John Jaruczky says, "The memory of those personal intimate moments with Dr. Graham brings a gentle smile."

24

Thank You, Mr. Graham

Mary E. McQueen

Nine years old and alone on Sunday morning, I was sitting on a sidewalk in the Los Angeles slum where my daddy, mother and I lived. An elderly lady came over and sat down beside me. "Hello," she said, "my name is Anna. What's your name?"

"Mary."

"Would you like to go to Sunday school with me today?"

"Don't think my daddy would let me."

"Well, how about we ask him if you can go?"

I got up, took Anna's hand, and led her up three flights of stairs to our apartment. I opened the door. My dad was lying drunk on the couch, a cloth covering his eyes. When we walked over to him, he pulled off the cloth, and with an expletive said, "And who are you?"

Anna introduced herself and asked if I could go to church with her.

"I don't care. Take her with you. Just leave me alone."

Anna took my hand and we walked down the stairs and got into a shiny new car. I sat on the leather seats and thought I'd died and gone to heaven.

When we got to church, Anna took me to a room in the basement. I had never been in a church before. It was a very busy place, with lots of Sunday school rooms full of noisy children. Anna held my hand and went into the classroom with me. She introduced me to Miss Lee, the teacher, then I sat at a low table with several other children. I was worried she was leaving.

"I'll be right over here," she said and walked over to a chair by the wall. I kept looking at her, hoping she would not leave me alone. There was a lot of excitement about a movie they were going to show after Sunday school.

A bell rang, a lot like a school bell, and Anna took my hand and took me to a big room where there were all kinds of food on tables and juice and milk to drink. Anna sat with me while I scarfed down fruit and a donut. I had not eaten since the day before, and I was hungry.

Then we went into the big room full of people. They sang a lot of songs and a tall man in a fancy suit stood on the stage and announced, "Today the message will be brought by a new evangelist named Billy Graham. We have his sermon from the other night in downtown Los Angeles on film. Please turn down the lights and start the movie."

I had never seen a moving picture before, other than the boxing matches on a small black and white TV Daddy had been given for selling a car. Anna held my hand as we watched the movie. A young man with curly hair appeared on the white wall behind the pulpit. I could hear the machine clicking behind where we sat.

He was very excited as he talked. I didn't understand a lot of what he said, till he shouted loudly, "If you believe in Jesus Christ, your life will be better. Jesus will come into your life and make things better for you. If you want Jesus in your life, come down to the altar when this movie is over, and he will meet you here and come into your heart."

I looked up at Anna, who leaned over closer to me. I whispered, "Can I go up there, Anna?"

"Well sure you can, dear, and I will go with you."

She took my hand and we walked down the wide center aisle to the big stage where the pastor and others were waiting. The pastor leaned down to me, "Do you want Jesus to come into your heart, young lady?"

"Yes, I do. I want Jesus to come into my heart."

"What is your name?"

"Mary."

I felt Anna's hands on my shoulders. The pastor put his big hand lightly on top of my hand. "God, please come into Mary's heart and bless her and keep her safe in your hands all the days of her life. Amen."

I felt a surge of hope in my heart. Oh, how wonderful it would be if my life could change somehow! My daddy was drunk all the time. We moved every six months to keep ahead of his drinking. He beat my mom all the time. She was in the hospital a lot. I was always hungry. Sometimes the only thing we had to eat was what I could find in garbage cans. My daddy always told people who wanted to help us that he didn't accept charity."

Anna and another lady walked me to Anna's house where she served fried chicken, potatoes, biscuits and pie for lunch. I was so full I almost felt sick. The two ladies packed chicken, potatoes, biscuits and pie into a box and set it on the back seat beside me, then Anna drove me home. She carried the box and walked with me up the three flights of stairs. My daddy was still lying on the couch, the cloth over his head.

"What do you want?" He didn't take the cloth off his head.

"Anna brought me home from church and she sent chicken and biscuits . . . and . . . ."

He rose up angrily off the couch. "I don't take charity!" He took the box from Anna and threw it in a garbage can in the kitchen. "Now get out of here! Mary, you go to your room!"

"Can Mary go with me to church next week?"

"I don't care, just leave me alone."

"I'll pick her up at 8:00 then."

He lay down on the couch and Anna left. I later dug the food out of the garbage and hid it in my room so Mama would have something to eat when she came home."

The next week, Anna came at 8:00 and drove me to church. The pastor came in during Sunday school and talked about how people who believed in Jesus needed to be baptized. I was excited as we put on white robes and went to the back of the big stage where the pastor stood in a pool of water. I went down the three steps and the Pastor asked me in front of everybody if I believed in Jesus Christ. I told him I did, and he had me put my hands over my face and he gently leaned me back into the warm water.

"I baptize Mary in the name of the Father, Son and Holy Ghost."

I felt excited all over. Anna told me Jesus was in my heart. And, somehow, I changed that day from a hopeless little girl to someone who knew Jesus was going to make my life better. During the next six months, Anna came every Sunday morning and took me to Sunday school and church and served me a meal afterwards. It was the only full meal I ate all week.

One day I awoke to my mother's screams. Several policemen were there. They took my daddy away and my mother left in an ambulance. This cycle of Daddy's violence, moving to another place, and more violence continued for about five more years. My mother had no saleable skills but finally was helped to get to her family in another state.

I began to learn there was a better way to live. Jesus, and Mr. Graham, had kept their promises. During those five years, I often talked to Jesus and asked, "When, Jesus?" I didn't understand why, but when I talked to Jesus, things were already better inside me.

But the best fulfillment of the promise was yet to come. One day, a young Christian man came into my life. He had been raised in a totally different way. We married and over the years he showed me that faith in Jesus Christ does, indeed, result in a better life. A life filled with hope. The same message Mr. Graham told me about the first time Anna took me to church.

I have had the awesome privilege of sharing that message of hope for thirty years as an ordained pastor and Christian writer.

Thank you, Mr. Graham for your part in God's message to me. I am a life that was changed because you came with a message of hope.

25

Turning the Knob for Billy

Vicki H. Moss

When I was a young girl and my mother turned the knob of our television to search for the latest Billy Graham revival, I must admit I left the room moaning and sighing when I heard Billy preaching. "Really? I was into my show! Do we have to watch this?"

I never thought of Mother as a highly religious person though she curled my hair every Saturday night and dressed me fashionably for church every Sunday; which included black patent Mary Janes, white gloves, and a red rosebud from the front porch trellis on Easter mornings.

Though Mother was diligent in making sure her little chickadee was afforded the opportunity to hear "Just As I Am" and "I Surrender All" sung at the end of a sermon on a regular basis, the Bible was rarely discussed at home when I was growing up, so therefore, I couldn't understand what Mother saw in Billy Graham. Evidently, Mother's quiet faith was a lot like Queen Elizabeth's, another who favored the fiery sermons of Graham.

Not only was Billy's preaching too loud, so were his ties and argyle socks and they shouted the gospel with him even louder from sawdust trails during tent revivals and also from the constructed stages of humongous stadiums. So why would anyone join the masses to go sit through one of his fiery harangues to be told they were "wicked and sinners all?"

Since I didn't appreciate his preaching style, and his sermons were not the type I could sit through, I retreated to my bedroom and played with Barbie dolls or continued reading *Black Beauty*. Before becoming a mature Christian, there was no way I could comprehend the draw to this North Carolinian's enormous revivals. Even Billy's wife, Ruth Graham, was quoted as saying her husband's delivery was too loud. Amen sister.

Not until many years later did a friend share about her experience at The Cove — a retreat center built by Graham to bring people together in the mountain wilderness near Asheville, North Carolina to learn more about God from visiting Bible teachers and evangelists. With the friend's revelation, and during an especially dark night of the soul after Mother's passing, I immediately knew it was time for me to take a closer look at Billy Graham.

"If I book a trip to The Cove will you go with me?" I asked her.

"Of course, I'd love to go back!"

Off we drove. The profound experience blew us both away. Not only was the air crisp and invigorating, the fall mountains dazzled along with the excellent teaching provided by Jill and Stuart Briscoe. If all of the previously mentioned wasn't enough, the dining room smelled divine and provided lots and lots of ice cream with a nonstop cappuccino and hot chocolate machine where coffees and hot chocolaty treats could be enjoyed next to the huge fireplace or outside on the veranda while relaxing in one of the comfy rocking chairs.

At the end of the journey, I prayed in the Billy Graham chapel that housed a downstairs museum and was totally intrigued and ready to learn all I could learn about this fiery preacher. When I returned home, I borrowed my pastor's copy of Billy Graham's autobiography. The tome was thick, heavy, and unyielding in more ways than one and could be used as a deterrent against would-be-house-thieves and recalcitrant demons.

I wondered how I would ever manage to get through those pages. But read those pages I did — in between getting children to school, mucking out horse stalls, and applying flea prevention ointments to my wandering dogs and cats. Soon impressed even more with the man and his words, his personal convictions jumped to the fore. What would become known as the "The Billy Graham

Rule — a personal rule that he would not meet alone with a woman — convinced me this North Carolinian was a man of integrity . . . a man determined to carry out his mission for God, letting nothing stop him from spreading the gospel and helping save as many wicked sinners as he could reach, but also helping to bolster Christians who needed an encouraging message during difficult times.

From Graham's autobiography, I not only learned about the man, his life, and his incredible journey, I was also introduced to a couple of mentors Billy cherished — Henrietta Mears and Billy Sunday. Both stood out for me as well, and their Christian walks were stellar. Henrietta's book, *Dream Big*, is still one I keep close at hand and reread every year or two for motivation, along with Billy Graham's book on angels, *Angels: God's Secret Agents*. If I hadn't met Billy Graham through his own words, I wouldn't have been introduced to a score of incredible men and women he knew who also loved God and His Only Son and were willing to spend a life of servitude spreading the message about salvation and eternal life — all in the name of Jesus.

So, I owe a thank you to the man called Billy Graham, but a special thanks goes to Mother — a humble woman of quiet faith who loved hymns like "Just As I Am," and didn't hesitate to turn the knob to Billy so her child could surrender all.

26

Reach Out

Yvonne Lehman

When I was in my twenties, Billy Graham's radio message encouraged me to reach out to the world. I was busy within my world of church work, husband, and infant daughter, but I decided to volunteer a couple of hours a week at Shriner's Hospital. That led me to write an article for *Baby Talk* magazine about the blessing and appreciation of having a healthy baby. That was my first published article, although I didn't write it as a writer, but as a grateful mom.

In my thirties, after some disappointing events, I became disillusioned and considered leaving the church. Fortunately, after six months of pondering, I rededicated my life to the Lord, seeking direction. Then I noticed an ad in *Decision Magazine* about the Billy Graham School of Christian Writing. Attending that conference opened up a whole new world to me and I began my writing journey. That journey was not like singing and skipping along a yellow brick road, looking for a desired destination; it was trusting the Lord to be the light along my path, even when I could see no more than one step ahead at a time.

Eventually, my journey led to founding the Blue Ridge Mountains Christian Writers Conference where faculty reached out to thousands during the twenty-five years of my directing — and continues to do so now under others' direction.

Over the decades my journey has continued as more than fifty of my novels have been published. Then the nonfiction world opened up to me with the opportunity of compiling articles for the *Divine Moments* books, such as this one, and ten others now published. Hundreds of authors have shared their personal stories, humorous and serious. Readers have been entertained, faith has been strengthened, lives have been changed, and families have been reunited. All royalties from these books go to Samaritan's Purse, the organization founded by Dr. Graham's son, Franklin, an organization that provides spiritual and physical aid to hurting people around the world. Each writer is touching lives throughout the world, directly or indirectly.

Billy Graham's ministry has touched millions with one sermon. And yet, the preaching of one man led Billy Graham to surrender his life to the Lord Jesus Christ. What a difference one person can make in this world!

How blessed I've been by Billy Graham's life and words, beginning when I was just a young Mom and heeded the words God gave him.

His words reached me — one person — and all I had to do was surrender, take God's hand, and let him lead along the smooth or rugged paths.

God, through Billy Graham, has given me a blessed life I couldn't have imagined.

27

The Billy Graham Rule

Karen Sawyer

I never attended a Billy Graham crusade, in fact, before I became a Christian, I didn't give him much thought. After I became a Christian, I watched his crusades on TV every now and then but I had already accepted Jesus into my life, so they didn't have much effect on me. Don't get me wrong, I was thrilled to see all the people go forward to receive Christ. I admired his life and his ministry but neither made much of a difference in my own life. That is, not until until I heard about the Billy Graham Rule.

When I was in college, I worked at a Christian coffee house. In fact, my roommate and I lived above the coffee house and ran it as an outreach of our church. There were many times when only one of us would be working and single men would come into the coffee house to hang out. Sometimes they would stay for hours.

My roommate and I determined it wasn't good for either of us to be alone in that situation. Not all the men who came into the coffee house were Christians, and some were pretty rough around the edges. We discussed the situation with our pastor.

I'm not sure who, but someone mentioned that we needed to adhere to the Billy Graham Rule. That's when I was told that early in Billy Graham's ministry, he and his ministry team observed problems that other evangelists had encountered and how those problems had negatively affected their ability to preach the gospel. One of the things they noted was the constant temptation of sexual immorality while evangelists were separated from their wives and families for long periods of time during extended road trips. To avoid this, the men made a pledge to each other that they would never put themselves in a situation that may compromise the gospel, or even give the appearance of an indiscretion. From that day forward Billy Graham never allowed himself to be alone with a woman other than his wife. This included during meetings, meals, and travel.

My roommate and I immediately adopted the rule and from then on we always had another person in the coffee house when we worked.

The Billy Graham Rule stuck with me right into my own marriage. My husband and I have followed this rule as much as possible throughout our thirty-year marriage. We use it, not just in our marriage, but also in our business. We believe it's always best to have a witness or two at every meeting. While many people thought it was an extreme position for Billy Graham to take, it seemed like common sense to me. Why put yourself in a situation that, even if innocent, could be construed as something else?

Reverend Graham was not only looking out for his own reputation and his ministry, but he was being wise in the Lord. He was protecting all the women he met, those who were innocent of any malice and those who may have had other ideas.

Thank you, Billy Graham.

28

My Tribute

Colleen L. Reece

When I heard of Billy Graham's passing I couldn't help but see the parallel between his life and how much we can all learn from it. I chronicled a few facts to share on my blog for my friends and fellow authors.

America's pastor

Billy Graham achieved a position unlike any other evangelist. Respected and in touch with heads of foreign countries, he provided prayer and personal advice to a dozen USA presidents, starting with Harry S. Truman. An amazed world watched as the boy raised on a dairy farm in Charlotte, North Carolina, became "America's Pastor."

During his lifetime, Billy preached to an estimated 215 million people in 185 countries and reached millions of others via radio, television, and the internet.

An early calling

It was Easter weekend in 1937, Palatka, Florida. With knees knocking and four borrowed sermons to fall back on, eighteen-year-old Billy Graham delivered one sermon after another in front of the forty or so parishioners. He concluded his first career sermon eight minutes later!

He refused to be discouraged

After the service, one of the men at the church told Billy, "Boy, you better go back to school and get a lot more education."

Billy did. After wrestling with God, he eventually gave way to his calling to preach. His confidence grew with practice, even though his audience sometimes was nothing more than alligators, birds and cypress stumps, as he chronicles in his autobiography *Just As I Am*.

BILLY TOLD IT THE WAY HE BELIEVED IT

Being politically correct never kept Billy from speaking the words he felt God laid on his heart. Yet he appeared on Gallup's list of the most admired men and women sixty times since 1955 — every year the research company asked the question. Martin Luther King Jr. counted Graham as a close friend and ally, once remarking, "Had it not been for the ministry of my good friend Dr. Billy Graham, my work in the civil rights movement would not have been as successful as it has been."

HE NEVER USED "TOO BUSY" OR "I'M NOT UP TO IT" AS AN EXCUSE

Despite a schedule few of us could or would want to keep, Billy stole time to write more than two dozen books, books that required a great deal of research Although he was diagnosed with Parkinson's-like symptoms in the 1990s, his 1997 memoir, *Just As I Am*, was a *New York Times* best-seller.

BILLY GRAHAM STAYED FOCUSED

Married to Ruth Bell from 1943 to 2007 and father of five children, Billy's life's work required him to be away from home much of the time. He missed a great deal of time with his family, especially Ruth, of whom he said, "When it comes to spiritual things, my wife has had the greatest influence on my ministry."

29

Thirteen Pages

Tommy Scott Gilmore, III

I was in my twenties when God led me to accept a teaching and coaching position in Asheville, North Carolina. I knew of Billy Graham and his worldwide ministry but never expected our paths would cross even though he lived in the nearby area of Montreat.

I'd begun attending the Presbyterian Church on the campus of Montreat College. The college chaplain and senior pastor at that time was Dr. Calvin Theilman, who had served as special counsel to Dr. Graham and spiritual advisor to President Lyndon B. Johnson.

Dr. Theilman was preaching another one of his powerful messages. As usual, I was riveted on every word when my neighbor, Mrs. Anne Sharp Harrison, who served as a surrogate grandmother to me, leaned over and whispered, "Don't look now Tommy, but Billy, Ruth and the children are seated right behind us."

For a while I was unable to concentrate, knowing that great evangelist sat behind me. Dr. Theilman was a gifted preacher, and soon my thoughts were on the sermon and what it meant to be holy.

I always took a notebook to record Dr. Theilman's messages. I usually garnered three or four powerful illustrations. That day was different. I began writing everything unholy I had ever said, did or thought. The Holy Spirit was a vacuum cleaner, removing evil and wicked thoughts, spoken words, and mean or hateful actions I had committed.

I filled the first page in a few minutes then flipped it over and began writing on the back as memory after memory welled up.

After writing thirteen pages, I penned a personal note. "Dr. Graham, I am a friend and neighbor of Mrs. Harrison. She and your wife are friends. Here is a list of things for which I want forgiveness. I am a Christian but I want and need to be holy like you. I want God to use me. I'd like to meet with you for prayer. I know you're an incredibly busy man, but if you have a few moments, would you get in touch with me? Thank you. God bless you, Sir. In His love, Tommy Scott Gilmore."

I folded my thirteen pages, with the note on top, and turned around to hand it to Dr. Graham. The row was now empty. He and his family had left immediately after the invitation. I stood there, holding my thirteen pages.

As years passed, and I grew in faith, I worked with Billy Graham's staff in numerous ways. Initially, I met with Professor Charles Massey and Franklin Graham at the Graham home to discuss our summer itinerary for Rolling Vibrations Bicycling Ministry. We bicycled throughout Europe sharing our faith through singing and sharing our testimonies.

Franklin introduced me to Lowell Jackson, a staff member who handled student-related activities for Dr. Graham's crusades. Lowell and I worked together as I planned evangelistic outreaches for students in Asheville.

Lowell was responsible for anything pertaining to students at a Billy Graham crusade. He was also responsible for my being granted an interview with West End Baptist Church pulpit committee of Halifax, Nova Scotia, Canada, where I later became senior pastor.

Over the years, as I taught, preached, and worked with the BGEA staff in Asheville, Buffalo, Charlotte, Chicago, Halifax, Milwaukee, Montreat, and Raleigh, I formed a more understandable definition of what obtaining holiness really meant. Throughout the scriptures, there are references to holiness. To be holy means to be exalted or worthy of complete devotion as the one who is perfect in goodness and righteousness. It can also mean to be devoted entirely to God. Living for Christ is not about following a list of do's and don'ts. Nor is it about being gifted and using those gifts. It's about having a clean heart and mind and allowing the Spirit of God to live through a person.

Now, when I think of those thirteen pages of all my sins, mistakes and wrongdoings, it's as if God said, "Don't give your sins to someone else, Tommy. Give them to me. Only I can make you holy."

At a Sunday worship service at Montreat years ago, although I didn't meet Billy Graham personally, I met God personally in a new and different way.

I never got to pray with Billy Graham. What likely happened, while Billy Graham was sitting behind me, he was praying for me. That's the kind of thing a holy man does. He cares and prays for others.

Thirteen pages and an empty pew led to my life being spiritually impacted, and given opportunities I hadn't even known to ask for. Although Billy never read or answered my letter, God answered it for me, through Billy Graham's ministry.

30

Pray Like Billy

Cindy Sproles

Even as a child, I was captivated by this man who could awe thousands. I stood at the edge of the living room as my mother twisted the channel knob on the television.

"It starts at 7. Channel 5, I think." She turned the knob until the 5 glowed yellow. The picture tube slowly warmed, showing white static and fuzz on the screen. "Curt, adjust the rabbit ears. Hurry."

The camera panned across a stadium filled with people as the booming voice of George Beverly Shea belted out "How Great Thou Art." The song ended and Billy Graham stepped behind the pulpit. He clasped his hands tight and rested his elbows on the pulpit. His head bowed low, eyes squinted tight. "Heavenly Father, how great you are." And he continued to pray a touching and heartfelt prayer — an amazing faithful, confident prayer.

I heard the story of a theology professor who took his class of students to visit the home of Charles Wesley. The men meandered through the kitchen and living area, then made their way up the small staircase to the bedroom. Two worn spots in the middle of the bedroom floor led the men to discover these were where Wesley knelt and prayed daily. He prayed for the revival of the church.

Time slipped away and the men returned to the bus. Professor Orr began to take roll. One student was missing. He made his way back through the house looking for the student and as he climbed the stairs to the bedroom, a voice echoed through the hallway. There was the student, kneeling in the worn spots of Charles Wesley, praying fervently, "Lord, do it again. Please do it again. Revive the church."

Professor Orr gave the student a moment then gently tapped his shoulder. "Son, everyone is on the bus. It's time to leave." The young man came to his feet and walked to the bus. The student who joined his peers was Billy Graham.

I listened as Dr. Graham prayed across the loud speaker of the stadium, but what impressed this child was his prayer being so personal, so intent, that it seemed as though only he and God were in the stadium. His prayers were not for show, but heartfelt and inviting to the Spirit of the Lord. When he finished praying a curtain of understanding, newness, and yes, revival covered the venue. God spoke through His servant.

Listening to Billy Graham pray made a ten-year-old child long to talk to God that same way. Years have passed since my family showed up five nights in a row and tuned in to the Billy Graham Crusades on television, but nothing impressed me more than the fervent prayer of a true servant.

I've traveled to Black Mountain, North Carolina hundreds of times. I've hiked the mountain around the Graham home, often stopping, cupping my hand around my ear, hoping to hear the voice of this servant praying across the mountain. If I were to have the privilege of visiting the home of Dr. Graham, I feel sure I'd see worn knee prints in his floor.

The day Billy Graham prayed for God to do it again — revive the church — the Father heard his earnest plea and answered. For through the prayers of a faithful servant, hundreds of thousands came to know Jesus Christ.

When I think my prayers fall on deaf ears, I strive to remember the sincere words of a man who prayed without ceasing. He prayed waiting, expecting, believing God would revive the church. If I can emulate the mere determination to pray without ceasing, then I have learned from the master and I have the promise God hears . . . and answers.

Fifty years ago, a man walked to a pulpit, bowed his head, and prayed. God cleared the pathway for this servant so that a little girl heard his words and longed for that same type of personal relationship with Christ.

I never had the privilege to lay eyes on the real man, Billy Graham, but in one moment in time I learned to pray continuously, faithfully, and without fear. I learned that those moments in the early morning hours, when I couldn't sleep, were the times God nudged me to walk the hallway of our house and pray.

These days, I pick cards from my prayer bowl, holding them close to my heart and lift the names before the Lord. God doesn't require me to solve the issues of those for whom I pray, but He commands me . . . to simply pray.

I know when Dr. Graham entered the gates of heaven, God took him by the shoulders and turned him around to see the faces of all those he led to Christ. Hopefully, he saw the face of a ten-year-old little girl, who wanted to pray like Billy.

31

Accept or Reject

Helen L. Hoover

"If you don't make a choice to accept Christ tonight, then you are rejecting Him," Billy Graham emphasized at the end of his sermon on September 10, 1966. My husband was gone to work and our small daughter lay sleeping. I had the television on to pass the time and provide noise in the quiet house. Dr. Graham's statement pricked my heart. I'd gone to church as a child and had been presented with the gospel message of salvation, but I'd kept putting off my decision. It had never occurred to me that I was rejecting Jesus. I was just putting off accepting Him until a later date.

That night, at age twenty-three, I knelt in our bedroom and made the most important decision of my life. I immediately regretted not doing it years earlier. I hadn't been what the world considered a bad person with drugs, adultery, and drinking, but my life was miserable due to shame, anger, regret, and being unforgiving and critical of others. With my decision, the peace of knowing Jesus as my Savior and the hope of eternal life with Him flooded my soul. My life changed for the better and led to more good choices over the years.

I started attending church regularly. One Sunday, my pastor related a story about a lady who led each of her children to Christ while they were still small enough to sit on her lap. I took this to heart. I didn't want my children waiting until they were adults to accept Christ as their Savior, as I had done.

"God, please help and guide me to lead my children to You while they can still sit on my lap," I prayed.

God faithfully answered that request. As I sang hymns and read

Bible stories to each child over the following years, I watched for opportunities to explain Christ's death on the cross and their need for a Savior. They listened eagerly as I told them of God's love. Our three children had asked Christ into their lives as Savior by age six. I'm thankful God gave me the privilege of praying with each one when they made this important decision.

My husband, Larry, had gone to Sunday school as a child and knew the plan of salvation but had not accepted Christ into his life. His Christian mother prayed regularly for him and talked with him about Christ before and after our marriage. Excitement filled her, when I turned my life over to Christ. She knew another person now prayed regularly for her son.

The fulfillment of prayers for Larry came fourteen years later. "I know it is the result of my mother's and wife's prayers that I accepted Christ at age thirty-eight," he says. "Children are more receptive to accepting Christ than adults, but no one is ever too old."

Throughout the years, Larry and I have willingly helped in the churches we've attended. We enjoyed leading a youth group, directing the adult social activities, and singing with a worship team. Larry helped renovate a church sanctuary and taught a Sunday school class. I worked as a church secretary, helped with Vacation Bible School, and taught Bible study classes. For eight of our retirement years, we were members of Sowers, a volunteer ministry for RV owners who travel to various ministries across the United States and give practical help — carpentry, plumbing, sewing, office work, landscaping, painting, and electrical.

Our life has not been without challenges, but God has been faithful to help, direct, comfort, love, and guide us through each event. A fifteen-year-old son developed diabetes, an unwed daughter gave birth to a delightful granddaughter, a depressed twenty-three-year-old son shot himself and died. Christian friends have been invaluable as they've encouraged, listened, and walked with us through each hurtle that came our way.

Each November for the past fifteen years Larry and I have

donated between two and twenty-six filled shoe boxes to Operation Christmas Child with Samaritan's Purse. We are delighted to help in a small way so that others will be presented with the opportunity to accept Christ into their lives. It is fulfilling to realize that my Christian walk started with the Billy Graham ministry and now fifty-two years later, I'm helping the ministry.

Our life is blessed — all because of God's love and provision that became ours when we accepted Him as our Savior.

32

LOCKED OUT!

Suzy Liggitt

I thought we had left Pasadena in plenty of time to get to the Los Angeles Coliseum. As we parked our car, the lot was full but no one was walking toward the entrance. Were we late? I rushed ahead of my husband and his mother to get to the gates. I reached to pull them open. They didn't budge.

I threw my hands to the sky, "They're locked. We can't get in. The guard said they're full to capacity. No one else can get in."

My eyes stung from trying to hold back the tears. I didn't want my mother-in-law and husband to know how disappointed I felt. I had been searching to find just who God was. When I read about the Billy Graham Crusade coming to the LA Coliseum I desperately wanted to go. I thought I might find the answer to who God was and how I could know Him.

We rode home in silence. I knew my husband and his mother really didn't understand. At this point my life seemed to be spinning out of control. I tried everything to fill the empty void within me. I developed a singing career that seemed exciting at first, but now it brought on pressure that I found difficult to handle.

I knelt by my bed that night and cried out to the God I wanted to know, "I'm trying to find out who You are and how I can get in touch with You. I've cried out to You over and over. If you're there, please, please get in touch with me."

A few months passed and my husband announced that he had been transferred to the Orange County Office.

"Please," I said, "can we try church when we move? Maybe we can find the answers for meaning in our lives."

Two weeks after we moved into our new home we visited a

church nearby. Just like the Coliseum, the parking lot was full. We watched as people poured into the church. I feared they would close the doors before we could get in. We did get in, of course, but the seats had filled quickly.

We finally found seats. I felt mesmerized by the music and the words from the minister. He talked about a God who loved us and was interested in our individual lives. He told how God was perfect and absolutely holy. Because of the sin in our lives this Holy God couldn't have a relationship with us. My heart sank.

Then he said God had provided a solution and that was why He sent His Son Jesus to die and pay the penalty for our sin. When Jesus died on that cross He was paying the price for our sins. He paid the rap for us so that we could be free. All we had to do is receive this gift of salvation by inviting Jesus into our hearts and now be connected with the Holy God.

Tears streamed down my cheeks as I accepted this gift. No more locked gates. I could be free. I could be a new person in Christ. At last I had found the answer for the emptiness in my life.

Years passed and our church received the news that Billy Graham was coming to Orange County to hold a crusade and all the churches were invited to participate. I was a singer so I signed up to sing in the choir. What a thrill to practice songs with hundreds of other Christians under the leadership of Cliff Barrows.

The night of the crusade, Billy came to the podium and gave the message I had heard years before of God's love for us and how we each could be free of sin and death by receiving His gift of salvation.

Each night, when he invited the audience to come forward to receive God's gift hundreds of people filled the field as we sang "Just As I Am." Each night of the crusade I cried for joy and thanksgiving that all these people were hearing the message I had longed for on that night many years before when I thought I had been locked out from knowing God.

God had heard this lost and hurting young woman's prayers and opened His eternal gates in His timing and His way.

33
Back to the Basics with Billy

Kim Peterson

When Billy Graham changed his address from a rural route in western North Carolina to streets paved with gold, hundreds of thousands of people reflected on his life's impact. I'm no exception, though I never met the man.

As a little girl singing along to the music of his TV crusades, I had no idea how his message would eventually touch my life.

I grew up within a conservative denomination, but when it came time to choose a college, I attended a school of a different denomination. While this experience broadened my horizons and strengthened my knowledge and faith, I still held on to a narrow understanding of Christianity and its adherents.

I graduated from college and planned to return for a fifth year. But a special one-year intensive master's degree opportunity came to my attention at Wheaton College in Illinois. With only two weeks until the fall semester began, a college friend recommended a place to live until the room I rented became available.

Day after day, I hoofed it to the Billy Graham Center where my grad school courses took place. My professors belonged to a mix of denominations. None of their beliefs and practices resembled how I was raised. Immediately immersed — almost drowning — in rigorous academic courses, I met students from around the world and many segments of Christianity. I soon recognized my fellow communication majors were quite committed to Jesus Christ, yet very different from me.

Each day generated a new revelation that makes me smile now, but stunned me at the time. Missionaries were being sent to America from other countries! I attended school with ministers fleeing unrest where they served. Not everyone was a Calvinist!

My temporary five-week stay with a pastor's family exposed me to more faith traditions of which I had been unaware, but the move to my permanent housing really opened my eyes — wide. Icons lined shelves and perched in various nooks and crannies. Weren't those idols?

My landlady set me straight. These were precious treasures of the Russian church, smuggled out years earlier for safekeeping until they could be returned to the surviving Christians there.

What were they doing in a modest home in a Chicago suburb? Her father, a preacher and author, had been the smuggler.

During my time at Wheaton, I was exposed to liturgy, new-to-me interpretations of Scripture, and contemporary Christian music with a beat. Even the behaviors of some leaders shook me. A noted Christian author visited as writer-in-residence that year, yet he used a curse word in his latest novel.

My head was spinning and my heart found it all shocking. Near the end of my first semester, I was weary, overwhelmed, uncertain. My faith seemed so limited, yet the others seemed so liberal. Where did I belong? What was right?

I shared my mixed emotions and jumbled brain with a godly woman at work, a receptionist who encouraged me daily. She recommended that I visit the BGC Museum. What museum?

Apparently, I had climbed to the second floor every day for classes without realizing I was rushing past the Billy Graham Center Museum on the main floor. Not sure what good a tour would do, I heeded her advice anyway. During a break between classes, I went downstairs and wandered inside.

I discovered the exhibits focused on evangelism in North America. As I walked through displays about the giants of the faith, I encountered names I recognized from history: Jonathan Edwards, George Whitefield. As I moved into more recent history, I visited Dwight L. Moody, Billy Sunday and other names that meant a lot to me.

And I found Billy Graham.

As I read about his ministry and the droves of people who met Jesus through his preaching, I was struck by how simple, how basic, he kept his message.

Tears trickled from my eyes as I considered how the varying doctrines of the faith, the differences in worship styles, and the theology I didn't understand had overwhelmed me. Though important, none of them mattered without the Truth proclaimed by Billy Graham and those who had ministered before him: We all need the forgiveness that comes from inviting Jesus Christ into our hearts to be our Lord and Savior.

I had asked Him as a young girl. I believed in Jesus, loved Jesus, and lived for Him. Warmth enveloped me as joy replaced my anxiety. Hope and courage rose up within me. In that moment in the BGC Museum, reading the words of Billy Graham, I reconnected with the basics of my faith.

And I found God's peace.

34

A Sunday Afternoon

Roger Bruner

The closest I ever saw Billy Graham was from far up in the coliseum stands in Baltimore, when a group from my church went to hear him preach there while I was in my late thirties. But I felt a lot closer to him than that because of something that had happened years earlier.

Working on the 1968 summer staff at Ridgecrest Conference Center in western North Carolina, I couldn't miss the fact that I was in the heart of Billy Graham country. But I was too busy sweeping and straightening the auditorium and its adjacent buildings to even think about the possibility of meeting Dr. Graham.

The auditorium's public-address system — a very basic and undependable one compared to the complex system the current auditorium has — was operated by a crew of one. But he was assisted by Mr. Scott, who worked at WFGM, Billy Graham's radio station in nearby Black Mountain. I didn't even know he owned a station until then. The auditorium crew got to know Mr. Scott fairly well.

Before long, he learned that I sang and played guitar and was interested in folk music, which was all the rage at the time. He asked if I'd like to write and record an ad jingle for the Atlas Tire Company.

I couldn't pass up an opportunity like that. Although I've long since forgotten the words I set to "When Johnny Comes Marching Home Again," Mr. Scott was pleased, and he took me to the station one Sunday afternoon to record it.

When we went into an empty studio to do the taping, he told me that Billy Graham had used that same studio for his radio devotionals. Now *that* was interesting.

Recording the commercial didn't take long, and we were soon headed back to the conference center. I was still thinking about the fact I'd actually used the same studio Billy Graham had used. But I didn't dwell on it for long.

Nonetheless, it was an extra-special event, and the more I've thought about it since then, the more it's meant to me.

I occasionally wonder if Billy Graham ever heard my commercial and maybe even asked Mr. Scott who in the world had done that silly jingle. And whether Mr. Scott told him I'd done it at no cost to the station. Could Dr. Graham possibly have realized that had been my one special, but tiny and very indirect contribution to his ministry?

I've read Terry Whalin's book about Billy Graham and Patricia Cornwell's book about Ruth Bell Graham, Billy's wife. I haven't found any mention of my jingle in either of them. And that's a good thing.

I'll bet Billy Graham would've wanted it that way if he'd been in my shoes.

35

One Sunday Morning

Karen Lynn Nolan

I rose early one Sunday morning in 1968, before the rest of my family. I raised my window blind to find the fog still hugged the mountains surrounding my eastern Kentucky house. Chill bumps popped up on my arms from an early spring cold spell. I jumped back into the bed and snuggled under a blanket. Then I reached for the Bible I kept on my bedside table.

My parents didn't go to church, but Daddy often sat in front of the TV and watched the Billy Graham crusades. I had gotten into the habit of sitting with him and listening to the stories. I especially liked the ones where Mr. Graham told us God loved us. I needed to hear about being loved because no one had ever spoken those words to me in my fourteen years of life. At the end of the program, someone told us we could get our own copy of the book Billy Graham held in his hand and read from. Free for the asking. I grabbed a pencil and paper to write the address. The next day, I sent a letter to Billy Graham asking for my very own Bible.

After the package arrived in the mail a few days later, I read from my Bible every day — even the parts I couldn't understand. Usually, I read from John, Luke, or Mark. That spring morning, I opened to the front where salvation was explained. I read it twice to make sure I understood.

My heart knew what I needed to do. While sitting on my bed, I laid the Bible on my lap, clasped my hands, and whispered the Prayer for Salvation, so my family couldn't hear me. We didn't talk about spiritual things in my house. I asked forgiveness for all the sins that weighed heavy on my young, but troubled, soul. When I asked Jesus to come into my heart, happy tears bubbled from my eyes.

To make it official, I filled in the blanks on the next page. The day I prayed the prayer: May 5, 1968.

Knowing my inclination to be shy, I fashioned a plan. I dressed, ate my breakfast, and rushed out the door. My friend, Elizabeth, had convinced me to go to church with her the summer before. The small group of people, including the pastor, were now like family to me. I practically ran the mile to the yellow block church, my heart thumping more from excitement than the exercise. Out of breath, I burst through the front door, and marched down the aisle to where our pastor prepared for the service.

I blurted, "I prayed the prayer this morning and I plan to come forward during the invitation song." I felt a big smile spread across my face as I stood, not knowing what to do next. Brother Bob hugged me. His smile matched mine. I took my place on a pew and waited. My body refused to be still.

As a shy, naïve, introverted mountain girl, I tended to avoid public displays for attention. I had read what came after the prayer. The part about baptism scared me. I couldn't swim because of my fear of water. But I knew I needed to be obedient and since I told the pastor first thing, I couldn't back out when the invitation music started.

When the time came, my heart fluttered so much I thought I might throw up or pass out. I took a deep breath, then prayed for God to help me take the first step. Before I knew it, I stood at the front of the church, with a smile that made my face hurt.

My life changed that day. I began a journey I never imagined possible. The world around me didn't change and problems and challenges didn't disappear, but a transformation began in me. No matter what happened or didn't happen, I knew God promised to love me. That spring morning, I couldn't comprehend the impact my decision would have on my life. It took years to appreciate God's promise to never leave me nor forsake me. It took a lifetime to believe His promise to love me just as I am.

Billy Graham changed my life by telling me about Jesus. I

longed to return the favor some day and give back to his ministry. In September 1993, my chance arrived. News came that he would present a crusade in Columbus, Ohio, my home city at the time.

With a degree in music and several years as a church music director, I joined the crusade choir, under the direction of Cliff Barrows and with George Beverly Shea.

I also entered the chaplaincy training program a few months before the crusade. What joy when my fellow chaplains and I left the stands after the service to greet the hundreds of tearful people seeking prayer, guidance, and salvation.

Although I trembled with a sense of inadequacy, I trusted God to lead me through the process. What an honor to be a living duplication of the Plan of Salvation I had read in my Billy Graham Bible twenty-five years earlier when I accepted Christ. I cried with the people who came to me as we prayed together.

I am only one person whose eternity was changed by Billy Graham's love for Jesus and lost souls. Just one. But can you imagine how many "ones" like me will join him in heaven?

Oh, how I long to draw lost souls to the Lord as Billy Graham did. Even just one.

36

Words of Wisdom

Ann Knowles

Growing up on a small farm in rural North Carolina in the 50s was a wonderful life. Daddy farmed and worked with the local electric co-op. Money was often scarce but love abounded.

Mama taught me to love books as she read the classics to me when I was six years old. However, reading material was mostly limited to the Bible and a couple of Christian magazines.

I asked Jesus to come into my heart when I was thirteen. I studied the Bible and my Sunday school lessons diligently. I couldn't get enough of God's Word, and wanted to know more. I absorbed every word of *Home Life* and *Decision Magazine*.

Billy Graham wrote a question and answer feature each month in *Decision Magazine* which offered words of wisdom to this young Christian girl. People of every race, creed, and age wrote in with their questions, and he always answered succinctly, sometimes with humor, always with wisdom.

I distinctly remember once when someone wrote, "I want to do what Jesus wants me to do, but sometimes I'm not sure if things are right or wrong. What should I do?"

His answer was brief and to the point. He wrote, "When in doubt, don't!" It was like God had spoken directly to me.

Billy Graham would never know how those words molded my life. I made them my motto, and to this day I still live by them. They have served me well in making wise choices about all kinds of moral issues and in raising my four children to practice them.

When my grandchildren ask, "Grandma, do you think it's wrong to ____?" I respond, "When in doubt, don't!" Then I tell them about Billy Graham's impact on my life.

I was privileged to attend the Billy Graham crusade in Berlin, Germany, and was trained by Cliff Barrows to be a counselor. But no contact ever impacted my life like those first words of wisdom.

I have shared these words with hundreds of men and women as I have spoken at writers' conferences, in churches, and before civic groups. People are amazed that after all these years, I still remember them so vividly, but when I think about the world we live in, I realize how powerful these words are, and how much they are needed.

I will be forever grateful for this great man of God for sharing his words of wisdom directly and honestly with millions of people who were sincerely seeking the truth.

Do you sometimes ask yourself the question, "What would Jesus do?" and then have difficulty figuring out the answer?

Take Billy Graham's advice, "When in doubt, don't!"

37

His Continuing Influence

Diana Flegal

Here in the Asheville area we still grieve the loss of Billy Graham long after the rest of the world has moved on with their lives. We drive on the Billy Graham Parkway on an almost daily basis, pass the Billy Graham Training Center located in east Asheville where many of us have visited; either attending a Christian Writers Conference, or Bible study led by a Graham family member, or having enjoyed a five star Christmas buffett where one is sometimes served dessert by Gigi Graham.

And when visiting Black Mountain, we also know we are not far from Montreat, Billy and Ruth's longtime home.

I grew up listening to Billy Graham on TV and, when I was young, attended a Billy Graham crusade in my hometown, Johnstown, Pennsylvania. I can't recall a time when I was without the influence of Billy and his family. Just hearing his voice evokes a positive Pavlov's Dog response in me. I know I am in for a message full of inspiration and truth. A favorite book of mine was Ruth Graham's book of poetry and short vignettes, *Sitting by My Laughing Fire*. When my dog chewed it up, he almost lost his happy home.

Since Billy's passing, I have listened to his messages on Youtube, including intimate times he ministered from his bedside, praying for us all.

Now reunited with his loving wife Ruth and face to face with his Savior, heaven is rejoicing and we are here wondering how the favor we have enjoyed in western North Carolina will change with the passing of our warrior. How many will it take to shoulder his mantel? I for one, am challenged to reconsider my reach for the Easy button. Until there is no breath in me, I will seek to share the love of God, the good news Billy shared around the world. And some day, I will hear as Billy surely has, ". . . welcome home! Well done, good and faithful servant!"

38

A Special Memory

Fred Robinson, Jr.

For a week during May 1975, I was excited and privileged to be a part of the Billy Graham crusade choir held in Jackson, Mississippi. It was a once-in-a-lifetime opportunity which I will never forget.

The crusade choir was led by Cliff Barrows. Members were assembled from many local churches. I recall we had brief rehearsals prior to the crusade each night. Also, I will never forget special solo music by George Beverly Shea most evenings. The music from such a large choir was inspiring and uplifting. The trademark invitation song was always, "Just As I Am." I kept my crusade choir folder as a reminder of this wonderful occasion.

During the sermon, Billy Graham captured the audience's attention. He was a powerful preacher who was obviously ordained by God. His sermons appealed to everyone and many came to know the Lord that week. He preached as a friend to all, local or in a distant part of the world, proclaiming the good news of forgiveness of sins and the benefits of becoming a follower of Christ.

Whether on television or in person, Billy Graham was always the same — sincere, powerful and a true servant of God.

Music was an important part of each Billy Graham crusade. Who could ever forget Ethel Waters singing, "His Eye Is on the Sparrow" or George Beverly Shea singing, "How Great Thou Art"? For all these reasons, I will always have a special memory of participating in a Billy Graham crusade choir.

39

Because It Takes More Than Bread

Beverly Varnado

Billy Graham has influenced me in many ways through the years, but none more so than in his encouragement to read the Bible.

I heard author, Jerry Jenkins, tell this story several years ago in a writing class. While writing *Just As I Am,* the autobiography of Billy Graham, Jenkins asked Graham what form he takes in searching the Scripture.

Graham responded that wherever he was in the world — his home, someone else's home, a hotel room, or anywhere, he leaves his Bible open so he notices it during the day. Each time he sees it he stops and reads a verse or a chapter and sometimes reads for an hour or so. He said that wasn't when he was preparing a sermon, but for his own spiritual nourishment.

Jenkins shared in class he looked over and sure enough, an open Bible lay on Graham's desk.

This story impressed me. What would be my response to the question, "What form do you take in searching scripture?"

I've used several different forms during the years, but was first influenced by Billy Graham.

In my early years of walking with the Lord, I often read *Decision Magazine*, the magazine of the Billy Graham Evangelistic organization. In it Graham said, "I used to read five psalms every day and that teaches me how to get along with God. Then I read a chapter of Proverbs every day and that teaches me how to get along with my fellow man."

I followed that advice for years, so no matter what else I was reading, I included Psalms and Proverbs.

For a long while, I used a Bible reading guide based on the New Common Lectionary. Other years, I read continuously through the New Testament.

In 2018, I found a plan for reading through the Bible in a year that doesn't involve being stuck in the hard-to-read Leviticus for several days. It has an epistle, law, history, psalm, poetry, prophecy, and gospel reading each week. I love the flow.

It doesn't matter what form our searching the scriptures takes. It matters only that we're searching them.

Graham said, "The Bible can change our lives as we read it and obey its teaching every day." In a video celebrating his ninety-ninth birthday, he offered this encouragement, "Make the Bible your source and your authority. Quote it frequently. Let its message be your message. Study it. Mediate on it. Memorize it. Trust its promises. The word of God itself has power."

Reading the Bible has certainly changed my life. I will often open its pages and find a word that speaks directly to a situation I am dealing with on that day. In times of desperation, I have even slept with an open Bible beside me. Because I have read the Bible, when faced with a crisis — like when I faced cancer or when my husband had a heart attack — scriptural words will drift into my mind bringing comfort and peace.

When Satan tempted Jesus to turn stones into bread, Jesus quoted from the book of Deuteronomy, *"It takes more than bread to stay alive. It takes a steady stream of words from God's mouth."* (Matthew 4:4 MSG)

Yes, it takes more than bread every day to live. If we long for that steady stream of God's words in our lives, reading the Bible every day is the answer. Here is the link for a fifty-two-week printable Bible reading plan: http://www.bible-reading.com/bible-plan.pdf. There are also many other kinds of plans which can be easily located with an internet search.

If you feel so led, use it and share it with someone else in memory of that amazing man of God, Billy Graham.

40

This World Is Not My Home

Debra DuPree Williams

Many years ago, in churches located in Dothan, Alabama area, I stood in a chair next to my sister, singing "This World Is Not My Home." I never imagined that many years later the lyrics would find their way around the globe in a quote by the revered evangelist, the Rev. Dr. Billy Graham. As our family gathered in front of our old black-and-white television set to watch as the young pastor delivered the gospel message, I had no idea that one day I would watch as televised funeral services for Dr. Graham made their way around the entire world.

I don't recall the first Billy Graham crusade my family viewed, but I know we never missed one of his televised services. I was five or six years old the first time I saw one of the crusades. That anointed minister delivered the sermon in words that even a youngster like me could understand. Hundreds, if not thousands, of people left their seats to go down front and accept Jesus as their Lord and Savior as the choir softly sang "Just As I Am." As I watched, my heart was stirred, and tears streamed down my face.

The moment Billy Graham left this world for the next, the celebration began in heaven. It is my guess that festivities are continuing as millions of people wait to greet Dr. Graham, telling him that if it had not been for his sharing the gospel message, they would not be there. I'm sure his family members, who arrived in heaven before him, have anxiously awaited his homecoming. I think they've moved to the background as their beloved Billy shakes the hands of those who wish to welcome him home. After all, that is what his family did here on earth. They understood the importance of the task, the *calling*, given unto their Billy.

If ever there was a servant called to spread the gospel message, who did so for as long, and as willingly, lovingly, and as passionately as Billy Graham, I don't know who it would be. We can all say, "Well, done, good and faithful servant."

What about you? Have you heard a Voice calling you? Have you stopped and listened? Have you taken steps to heed that Voice?

The Billy Grahams of this world are few and far between, but I hope that if you've heard God calling you to a specific purpose, you've taken steps toward that end. Perhaps you've been called to preach the gospel, or maybe you've been called to be a part of the worship team, or perhaps you have a gift that would make you perfect for the task of greeter. Maybe you've been called to teach, or to act, to be a doctor, or an attorney, to be a member of our military, or maybe you feel led to care for little ones.

I have many friends who've been called to be writers. They, as in all the callings mentioned above, come in all sizes and shapes, and they write all manner of literature, from Sunday school or Bible school curriculum, to devotions or Bible studies, to various genres of Christian world-view fiction.

My point is, they heard the call and they answered. If you feel you are being called, no matter what it is God is calling you to, I hope you will take that first step, *in faith*, and answer. You never know who or how many people's lives could be impacted by something you said or wrote, by a prayer you prayed, or by some action you took.

No matter who you are or where you are, when you walk through the Pearly Gates, the celebration in Heaven will be no less than the one given to Billy Graham. That's just the nature of God and His promises to those who believe.

After all, as the old hymn and Dr. Graham said, *this world is not my home*. When our time on this earth is over, all of Heaven will be there to greet us with *Welcome Home!*

41

WHY THE TEARS?

Ann Brubaker Greenleaf Wirtz

At 9:10 A.M. they should have been airing Greg Laurie's program, *A New Beginning*.

Because I often run errands at this time, I know 106.9 WMIT radio's morning format very well. But *The Light from Black Mountain, North Carolina,* our local Christian radio station founded by Billy and Ruth Graham in 1962, was playing music.

This particular Wednesday, February 21, 2018, I was on my way to McFarlan's Bake Shop in downtown Hendersonville to purchase several dozen doughnuts, our monthly "thank you" for the employees who work for my husband. As I neared the bakery, the song ended and was followed by a simple statement that Billy Graham had died and more information would be forthcoming within the hour.

Tears sprang to my eyes. They continued all day and throughout the week. Each time I heard a comment, or saw a program about him on television, emotion welled inside me and I became tearful.

The question began to taunt me. *Why the persistent tears?* This faithful servant of the Lord was ninety-nine years old. His life had been long and inspiring to millions. His global ministry had been enormously effective for God. On top of that, it was breathtaking to contemplate the moment this great and humble man came into the Lord's presence to hear what he had read many times: *"Well done, good and faithful servant . . . . Enter into the joy of the lord"* (Matthew 25:21 NKJV).

Yet . . . I cried. Why?

I knew heaven was his gain, but it seemed like earth's loss. It was sad realizing that Billy Graham was no longer nearby, just east down the highway and up the winding mountain road to Little

Piney Cove, his home for over sixty years. Their charming, rustic log cabin, with its grand history of refuge and inspiration, was conceived and created by his beloved Ruth to provide a respite from the world and a peaceful home in which to raise their five children. It would now be empty of the Graham family. It seemed the end of an era, and it was.

Day after day, tears sprang to my eyes the instant I heard Billy's name. I understood in one sense . . . but still I didn't. Why was I crying?

Although I was sorrowful, my heart rejoiced in the joy of his home-going. Billy was finally with the Lord. He was finally reunited with Ruth. He was with the others he loved, all because each had placed their faith in Jesus Christ for eternal salvation. They had embraced the astonishing truth, and claimed for themselves, John 3:16: *God so loved the world that He gave His only begotten Son, that whoever believes in Him should not perish but have everlasting life.*

On Thursday, March 1, WYFF News 4 from Greenville, South Carolina, aired a live broadcast of the solemn removal of Rev. Billy Graham's casket from the Capitol Rotunda in Washington, D.C., where his body had lain in state for seven hours on Wednesday. News anchor Michael Cogdill was quietly reflecting on this high honor and on Rev. Graham's amazing life, his testimony and powerful impact. He shared how Billy always spoke of God's love for us, and how it became the major emphasis of his ministry.

Again, tears welled and slid down my cheeks.

At that moment, my heart leapt as an answer to *Why the tears?* They had come unbidden from the core of my soul, so deep their meaning had been elusive. They sprang from my desperate need for Christ. Every comment about Billy Graham was a reminder of all the things in my life that had been confessed, forgiven and redeemed. Every word about Billy, what he had preached, had been a soul-reminder that God loves me, a sinner . . . and I cried.

Billy declared God's Word and asked us the question that Jesus asked Martha: *"I am the resurrection and the life. He who believes in*

Me, though he may die, he shall live. And whoever lives and believes in Me shall never die. Do you believe this?"

Martha's answer resounds through the ages, *"Yes, Lord, I believe that You are the Christ, the Son of God"* (John 11:25-27).

When our answer, too, is, "Yes, Lord, I believe," we are saved. This miracle of a redeemed heart is a gift of God. This was Billy Graham's unceasing message, boldly underlined by one of the clearest statements in the John 14:6: *Jesus said . . . "I am the way, the truth, and the life. No one comes to the Father except through Me."*

These were the words of Truth preached by Billy Graham, man of God. My tears made sense now. They sprang from the deep well of my redeemed and grateful heart.

To God be the Glory!

42

LIFETIME PURSUIT

Audrey Tyler

Billy Graham greatly influenced the world as an ambassador for Christ. Millions of people came to know Jesus Christ because they trusted him and his ministry. Dr. Graham encouraged millions, including me, to pursue the lifetime faithful behavior he exhibited. He demonstrated the qualities Paul instructed Timothy to pursue in 1 Timothy 6:11-12 (paraphrased).

1. Righteousness – Know the right thing to do and do it.
2. Godliness – Give proper reverence to God and the things of God.
3. Faith – Trust God for all things.
4. Love – Care for others more than self.
5. Steadfastness – The ability to endure
6. Gentleness – The willingness to handle others with care

My moments with Billy Graham are moments with his books. I came to know him through his writings. In my library are several books written by him. My favorite is *Angels*. His life and writings have led me to deeper trust and precious moments with God.

43

A Servant Leader

Joann Claypoole

"Well done my good and faithful servant . . . ."

Seven words every believer in Christ longs to hear from The Holy of Holies at the end of this life's journey must have rung so sweet that day. I can only imagine the look on Reverend Graham's face the moment he met Jesus.

That February morning, the sun shone bright, the air was crisp. My husband and I celebrated our twenty-ninth anniversary at our cabin in western North Carolina. Though winter had made it clear spring was not right around the corner, I listened to a melodic birdsong and watched several species nibble fresh seed from two feeders that hung on the porch railing. A tangled wind chime rang in the breeze, beckoning me to stop tapping computer keys for a

few moments. After I slid the glass door open and walked out to the back porch deck, I immediately pulled my phone from my pocket and snapped a photo when a beautiful rainbow arched across the sky.

Moments later, my husband walked out to tell me Billy Graham had passed. We admired the vivid colors and then hugged before it faded away. I immediately posted my photo on Instagram with this caption: *Caught a glimpse of heaven rejoicing this morning. Billy Graham, spiritual gift to the world, our loss is heaven's gain. I'm happy we'll meet again.*

God painted beautiful rainbows across the world that day.

Billy Graham is revered and remembered as the most significant evangelist the world has ever known. His sermons, broadcast on radio and television, are still rebroadcast today. The world watched him calm nations in times of war. He inspired leaders and celebrities with his humble heart, warmth and simple words of wisdom. He showed the world the way to love by following his heavenly Father's leading.

This speaker, teacher, and mediator won the respect of millions with his mild way — and inspired me with his quiet, yet confident demeanor, and especially with his words. I cherish *Angels, God's Secret Agents,* the first book I read by Dr. Graham. It touched my life with the realization of how God keeps watch over His children every day. It sits atop a prominent shelf in my library along with *The Secret to Happiness* and *Approaching Hoofbeats.* His inspirational quotes and poetic writings resonate in my soul and keep me coming back for new revelations again and again.

Through the years, I've enjoyed reading Ruth Bell Graham's love poems and stories. Through her beautiful poetry one can see how her loving husband inspired her writing journey.

In 2002, the musician-songwriter Bono (from the Irish rock band, U2) was inspired to write a poem for Billy after he visited the Graham family home in the mountains of western North Carolina. This hand-written poem is on display at the Billy Graham library in Charlotte, North Carolina.

I'm thankful to say Billy Graham impacted and influenced my life and my writing journey. I'm amazed to think how God used his faithful servant to move religious mountains and cross great divides, yet uses that same messenger to inspire the poet and inspirational writer in me. He said, "Come just as you are." And I ran.

The Word of God inspired Reverend Graham to lead us in the way of righteousness. This humble servant leader was and will always be an incredible inspiration in my life. I look forward to the day we meet. Then I'd like to thank him for the way he not only led, but followed in our Savior's steps.

THE WAY TO LOVE

The life of a man
Billy Graham
taught this world
the way to love.

Wisdom speaker
Simple man
Billy Graham
taught the church
the way to love.

He calmed the lions
with meekness of
the Holy Lamb
taught the nations
the way to love.

Servant leader
Humble man
Billy Graham
showed the world
the way to love.

44

MOTHER'S ANSWER

Penelope Carlevato

I was probably too zealous, but when I became a Christian, I thought everyone would want to join me, especially my mother. Sadly, this was not the case. She insisted I was already a Christian and even sent me a large box of my old Sunday school lessons to prove she was right.

As I went through the contents, I found no evidence that I had ever asked Jesus to be my personal savior. Thus began nine years of a limited relationship between our family and my mother and father. I promised God I would not talk about Christianity unless it was His idea.

Years went by. We all got along because my husband and I were passionate about our children having a loving relationship with their grandparents, so we kept quiet about our faith, and we prayed hard.

My English mother, a graduate of the Royal College of Music in London and an accomplished pianist, was invited to be a judicator for the National Music Teachers Association. That meant in addition to operating a large music studio she judged piano students all over the United States. We were thrilled when she was asked to judge close to our home in Denver.

She extended her time in Denver to spend a few days with us, and since her visit was over a weekend, she agreed to go to church with us.

During Sunday morning breakfast, Mother made several comments about how much she worked in her church, singing in the choir, teaching Sunday School and ironing the communion cloths. "This," she said, "is my ticket to heaven."

I felt that the Lord was saying, "Okay, now is the time." I shared Ephesians 2:9 which tells us we are not saved because of anything we do, but only because Christ died for us. This didn't go over well. She left the breakfast table and slammed the bedroom door. My young daughter said, "Well, I guess Grandma isn't coming to church with us."

We continued to get ready for church. I heard the bedroom door open and my mother asked Angela: "Would it be okay if I still went to church with you and Mummy?"

"Oh, yes, Grandma, I want you to come with us," replied my daughter.

The ride to church was very quiet. We got settled into our seats in the balcony and to my surprise we had a guest pastor. Not just any guest pastor, but a very distinguished Bible scholar from England. He captured my mother's attention and I was astonished when he spoke the following words: "If you think you are going to heaven because of all the wonderful things you have done, especially in church, such as teaching Sunday school, singing in the choir or helping with communion, you are sadly mistaken." He then repeated Ephesians 2:9. I looked over at my mother and noticed she was sitting up very straight and quiet.

As we were leaving the balcony, she whispered, "I should like to speak to that priest." We made our way down to the altar where he was meeting the congregation. I learned on the car ride home that she thought he was "all right," as he had preached in the very church in England where I had been christened many years earlier.

Later that afternoon we received a phone call that my father had taken ill, and my mother had to cut her visit short. The next day, my father was taken to the VA Hospital in Minneapolis, Minnesota, for medical tests. My mother went with him, and it just happened to be the same time that a Billy Graham Crusade was in Minneapolis.

Mother stayed at a boarding house close to the hospital and decided she wanted to go to the crusade. She called the church of her denomination and asked if anyone was going to the crusade and could they take her. "No, no one is going," she was told. The lady who ran the boarding house suggested they call the little Baptist church down the street. They were delighted to pick her up in the church bus each day. My mother went to the crusade for three days and on the last day she responded to Billy Graham's call for salvation. I received a call after she and my dad returned home, and she told me all about how she finally understood what I had been trying to tell her for many years. She told me she felt like Billy Graham actually knew her story and gave her answers she had never received before.

I was elated and asked her if she had talked to anyone after walking down onto the field or received materials to grow in her faith. "No," she said, I didn't want to miss the bus, so I didn't talk to anyone." After finishing our phone call, I called the Billy Graham Crusade office in Minneapolis and told them the story. Within a half hour, they had a volunteer at my mother's front door. She prayed with my mother and left her with several books and information and even had her signed up for a Bible study at a local church.

The transformation I witnessed in the next couple months was amazing. My mother went from a person who didn't believe you should talk about religion to joining an organization that went door-to-door sharing the gospel. She was also able to lead my dad to the Lord before his death several years later.

I will forever be grateful to Billy Graham for his ministry and for the transformation that I saw in my sixty-five-year-old mother.

45

Until Then

Diana Leagh Matthews

Billy Graham's funeral served as a beautiful reminder of the life mission and ministry of this humble man, who gave all the honor and glory to God.

The first song performed at his funeral, "Until Then," is a beautiful song reminding us to joyfully carry on in God's work until we "behold that Golden City."

While this was a new song to many, this was not a new song to me. I accompanied Daddy many times over the years as he performed this beautiful song. I've continued to sing it since his own homegoing.

What did surprise me was the many people who researched the song and posted their findings on my website where I share hymn histories each Sunday. Most amazing is, while Billy Graham was inspired by the lyrics in the song, the songwriter was brought to his knees and a relationship with God through a Billy Graham crusade.

"Until Then," sometimes referred to as "My Heart Can Sing When I Pause to Remember," was written by Carl Stuart Hamblen.

Hamblen was born on October 20th, 1908 in Kellyville, Texas. He was the son of a traveling Methodist minister. His career began in 1926, when he became the first singing cowboy on radio stations in Fort Worth and Dallas, Texas.

By 1931, he was on the radio from Hollywood, California as "Cowboy Joe." For the next twenty-one years, he had three radio shows that stayed at the top of the charts. They were: *Covered Wagon Jubilee, Stuart Hamblen and His Lucky Stars,* and *Cowboy Church of the Air.* He wrote numerous western songs for the radio, and began to star in motion pictures alongside well-known names such as Gene Autry, Roy Rogers and John Wayne.

In 1933, he married Veeva Ellen Daniels, whom he nicknamed "My Suzy." Hamblen became the first artist signed to Decca records in 1934. He made history in 1945, when he became the first man to fly his racing horse, El Lobo, on a plane. The horse won the race, and Hamblen flew him back home.

In 1949, Hamblin met evangelist Billy Graham and encouraged his listeners to attend the crusades being held in the area. Promising his wife, Suzy, he'd be there, he kept to his word. At the crusade, God began to knock on his heart. He tried to run away, but eventually he surrendered his life to God.

In the early 1950s, Hamblen's radio show was in national syndication when his sponsors tried to force him to allow the commercial promotion of alcoholic products. Hamblen refused, and his show was canceled, but not before Hamblen had the opportunity to witness to his listeners about why he was leaving the airways.

Always one for an adventure, he ran for President of the United States in 1952. He ran on the Prohibition Party and came in fourth to Dwight Eisenhower. He and Suzy lived on their ranch in Santa Clarita where they raised their two daughters, and watched the expansion of their family with grandchildren and great-grandchildren. On the ranch he bred Peruvian Paso Horses. Hamblen continued to produce his weekly nationally syndicated radio program, *Cowboy Church of the Air*.

Hamblen died on March 8,1989. He and Suzy were married for fifty-five years. She died on June 2, 2008 at the age of 101.

"Until Then" was originally published by Hamblen's publishing company in 1958. Hamblen wrote other hits including "It Is No Secret What God Can Do," "Teach Me, Lord, to Wait," and "Beyond the Sunset." He has been inducted into numerous Halls of Fame, including the Gospel Music Hall of Fame, Nashville Songwriters Hall of Fame, Western Music Hall of Fame, and he has a star on the Hollywood Walk of Fame.

"Until Then" has been published in at least four hymnals and various other songbooks and remains a song that reminds us of how glorious it will one day be to "behold that city when God calls us home."

Billy Graham shared how he looked forward to arriving in heaven. He is quoted as saying, "Someday you will hear that Billy Graham is dead. Don't you believe a word of it. I shall be more alive than I am now. I will just have changed my address. I will have gone into the presence of God."

He longed to go to heaven. And so should we. But, "Until then," we should learn from the life of Billy Graham that "with joy I will carry on."

That's what the Apostle Paul prayed, as recorded in Romans 15:13 — that the God of hope would fill us with all joy and peace as we trust Him, so that we may overflow with hope by the power of the Holy Spirit.

As we pause to remember the life and legacy of Billy Graham, we can carry on with joy and have a heart that is singing for the kingdom of God.

When we arrive in that glorious city, we will behold our Savior and Lord and can find a rock at the edge of a stream to sit and share with Billy all the ways in which he ministered to our hearts and drew us closer to God, such as his ministry touching the soul of Stuart Hamblin, and many others, including me.

46
A Special Sign

Debbie M. Presnell

I was in middle school with mostly seventh grade things on my mind. Schoolwork, friends, bike riding, and going to church were the standard activities that filled my schedule and occupied my thoughts. Although I was young, my pastor singled me out and invited me to take part in a new sign language class.

My church was beginning a ministry for the deaf community and being able to communicate with the deaf was important to our pastor and the church members. Training interpreters was also an urgent priority.

The pastor's asking me to take part in a class with adults made me feel special and chosen for an important task. So, I said yes.

Soon, I learned that signing was something I could do well. I had no trouble learning the signs and could readily understand what the deaf were signing to me.

The following year, when the deaf ministry formally began, I assisted as an interpreter during most Sunday morning services along with other interpreters. At first, I signed only the worship music. But eventually, I was able to interpret the sermon.

The deaf congregation was extremely supportive. They enjoyed helping me improve my talent and showed me interesting ways to express myself so they could understand the concept even better.

"We'll just read your face," they would sign.

Soon, I was labeled as the interpreter with the smile and facial expression that enabled deaf people to understand — regardless of what my hands were signing.

I couldn't have imagined what would happen three years later, when I was fifteen years old. Billy Graham would hold a revival in my city — Asheville, North Carolina. The entire city — including me — was buzzing with excitement and busy with preparation.

For several weeks I practiced the songs I would be responsible for signing. I carefully chose my outfit, too — modest in style and color, so the deaf wouldn't be distracted. When the time arrived, the Asheville Civic Center was filled to capacity. The deaf had a reserved section on the side mezzanine to the left of the platform, a perfect view for them to watch Billy Graham, the soloists, and the music leaders, while keeping the interpreter in view. While signing and observing onlookers reactions, I could see how deeply they were touched by his message. I felt a deeper presence of the Holy Spirit.

At the time I knew the event was important. But looking back as a mature adult, I am even more aware of how God blessed a young girl by prompting that preacher to ask her to learn sign language . . . and where that led. I realize what an honor, privilege, and responsibility to have been part of such an event — led by the most famous and influential evangelist the world has ever known.

Through that experience, God gave me a sign that he can combine a great man like Billy Graham, and a young girl, to accomplish his purposes.

I am so blessed. That experience stands out as one of the fondest memories in my spiritual journey.

47
World Changer

Dr. Rhett H. Wilson, Sr.

No human name received as much respect in our home as his. Growing up in my Southern Baptist home, we talked about many Christians, pastors, and ministries. Our family and church appreciated evangelists, missionaries, and soul-winning ministries. But no one held our admiration as much as Billy Graham.

He was America's pastor and a pastor to presidents. He believed God's Word was true, and in days when liberal theology crept into many mainstream denominations, Dr. Graham encouraged our belief system when he preached, "The Bible says."

Summer Sunday nights when I stayed at my grandparents' home, we drifted off to sleep listening to Billy Graham's voice coming through the clock radio above my grandparents' bed.

Growing up in the 1970s and 1980s, I vividly remember three times a year when the Billy Graham Evangelistic Association bought airtime the same week on CBS, NBC, and ABC and televised an evangelistic crusade. Life stopped in our home those evenings to hear Cliff Barrows and George Beverly Shea sing, well-known Christians share their testimonies, and the beloved Southerner share God's Word and invite people to come to Jesus.

Living in Greenville, South Carolina, also the home of Cliff Barrows, I thought it amazing to occasionally run into the Barrows on Sunday nights after church at local restaurants. They were real people just like us!

In college, I sent a small check to the BGEA and received *Decision Magazine* along with Billy's monthly letters, always including his personal underlining to emphasize key sentences. Some religion professors at my college believed in universalism — that God saves everyone. They did not emphasize revivalism, conversion, or the inerrancy of the Bible. Reading various biographies of Billy Graham encouraged me. I found strength in Billy's own journey as a young man to accept the Bible as literally true and trust God to preserve his own Word.

One of my dearest friends came to Christ through Billy's television ministry. As a teenager, Thomas watched a crusade at home. At the invitation, he knelt on the floor of his house and gave his life to Jesus Christ. Today Thomas trains missionaries to share the gospel in Muslim countries.

Two of my best friends from college and I decided to treat ourselves by attending the brand new Billy Graham Training Center at The Cove. We paid for our admission one summer weekend but could not afford to stay on campus. Instead, we planned to camp at a nearby campground. However, the first night we arrived back at the campground too late, and we had no place to stay. We returned to The Cove and explained our unfortunate situation to the security guard at the Welcome Center. A compassionate man, he told us we could sleep in our sleeping bags in the Welcome Center as long as we got out of there before anyone else showed up in the morning! We enjoyed a night on the floor and couches there. It was twenty-five years ago, but to this day I think about that night every time I go to The Cove. I expect we are the only three people in the history of the Training Center to camp out in the Welcome Center — and for free!

A print of the Chatlos Memorial Chapel at The Cove sits on my wife's dresser. It reminds us of countless visits to the Training Center, receiving excellent Bible teaching, encouragement, and refreshment.

During my seminary days, I studied and graduated from The Billy Graham School of Evangelism, Missions, and Church Growth at The Southern Baptist Theological Seminary in Louisville, Kentucky.

One of my mentors trained me to share the gospel using the "Peace with God" tract developed by the Graham organization. The Holy Spirit used that familiar bridge illustration to bring countless souls into the kingdom of heaven.

The past several years, we have enjoyed taking our children to the Billy Graham Library in Charlotte, exposing them to the rich heritage of a faithful Baptist preacher who touched the world.

Billy received harsh criticism from certain parts of the Body of Christ because of his open arms, open heart, and open mind. He didn't believe everyone had to believe exactly like him about everything in order to have a relationship with God. He thought they needed Christ. And he took every opportunity to introduce people to Christ.

I learned from Dr. Graham that if a person belongs to Christ, they belong to me. They may come from a different denomination, theological bent, or hold varying convictions, but if they believe in the authority of the Bible and the divinity of Jesus, and they have given their life to Him, they are my brother or sister. Dr. Graham did not try to be the Holy Spirit and change everyone. He learned to love them, to listen to them, and to lead them.

Dawson Troutman, founder of The Navigators ministry, once visited Wheaton College. Meeting a young, lanky William Graham, Dawson cornered him and asked, "Young man, what did God give you in His Word this morning?"

Graham stammered and struggled, knowing God did not give him anything that morning because he had not given any time to the Lord that morning in His Word. Young Billy Graham determined right there that never again, as much as it depended on him, would he not have a positive answer to that question. He would spend time with the Lord every morning.

Years later, when the Billy Graham Evangelistic Team formed, the men made several pacts. One such agreement was called "No bread, no bread." This phrase simply reminded them that they would not eat food each day if they had not first eaten from the Word of God. Feeding their souls with the Bread of Life trumped breakfast, lunch, and supper.

Billy Graham's name mirrors integrity, a life without a hint of scandal. His preaching remained forthright but simple, reflecting the veracity of the Word of God. His life exuded spiritual disciplines, anchoring him to the God he loved.

My father told me once, "Son, there will never be another Billy Graham."

I think that's true.

One of the gigantic figures of American evangelicalism, his simple faith, clear belief in the Bible's authority, and abiding love for Jesus and people propelled him to the nations. The young man from North Carolina changed the world.

48

Remembering Ruth

Yvonne Lehman

A book about Billy Graham would be remiss without the mention of his beloved wife, Ruth, the love of his life. She was also a beloved woman, author, speaker, influence to the world and to our local community of Black Mountain and Montreat, North Carolina. Whenever I heard Rev. Graham's daughter, Gigi, or his grandson, Will, speak at The Cove after her death in 2007 they never ceased to mention how much Billy missed her, and longed to be with her.

She was well-known for her commitment to prayer. This was emphasized on June 1, 2016 at the dedication of Ruth's Prayer Garden held outside the Chatlos Memorial Chapel at the Billy Graham Center at The Cove in Asheville.

The impact the Billy Graham ministry had on my life prompted me to *give back* and volunteer some of my Saturday mornings for leading tours in the Chapel. As a volunteer, I was invited to attend the dedication. Over 150 people attended, outside the chapel, facing the beautiful garden.

Gigi Graham and Yvonne at the dedication of Ruth's Payer Garden.

Will Graham, Ruth's grandson and Franklin Graham's son, gave a tribute to his grandmother and spoke about the three gardens of the Bible: Eden, Gethsemane, and the new one written about in

Revelation. We sang Ruth's favorite song, "In the Garden." This was printed on the program:

Ruth's Prayer Garden . . .

Consists of two tiers. The garden is planted in large sweeps of woodland shrubs and perennials, with large open areas for ground cover. Almost every plant in the garden blooms in one way or another.

The garden is meant to provide a place of solitude and beauty for the purpose of personal reflection, prayer and worship.

As you stroll through the garden, you will see a mix of perennials and roses, planted in front of the chapel in the English style of perennial gardening. The colors and textures of the plants contrast and soften the stone of the chapel and are intended to be a small replication of the great gardens found around churches in England.

The variety of plants also reflects the botanical tastes and interests of the Bell family as well as the Grahams. Many of Ruth's favorite plant species are included in the garden including daylilies, daisies, coneflowers and roses.

Being a part of that occasion, aware of the overwhelming beauty of such a place — all of God's creation really — thinking of the lives changed through the ministry of Billy Graham, and Ruth Graham's ministry of prayer, I felt honored to be able to volunteer a few hours. The first time I entered that chapel, gave a tour in that gorgeous place, feeling the spirit of the Lord in a special way, I knew I was receiving more than I could ever give.

I can only thank God for the awesome privilege of being loved by Him.

My heart sings the words of a song we sang that day as I walked through that garden:

> When through the woods,
> And forest glades I wander,
> And hear the birds sing sweetly in the trees,
> When I look down, from lofty mountain grandeur
> And see the brook, and feel the gentle breeze,
> Then sings my soul, My Savior God, to Thee,
> How great Thou art, How great Thou art!

Ruth Graham was buried at the foot of a cross-shaped walkway in the prayer garden on the grounds of the Billy Graham Library in Charlotte, North Carolina, the birthplace of Billy Graham. He died at the age of ninery-nine. As they agreed, he was buried beside his wife.

However, upon his death February 21, 2018, Billy Graham was immediately ushered into heaven and reunited with the millions whom his ministry won to Christ, and his friend George Beverly Shea who sang "How Great Thou Art" so many times.

But even more exciting is the thought that this man, who meant so much to the world, and to one individual at a time, is now with those he loved most — his beloved wife Ruth, and Jesus.

49

HAPPY GRADUATION BILLY GRAHAM

Joye Atkinson

Happy graduation Billy Graham!
You're now with the King of Kings
Transported to his presence
carried up on angels' wings.

Your life on earth has ended,
and even though we're sad,
You are reaping your great harvest
and for that we are glad.

We can see you walking with the Lord
down the streets of gold
Reunited with Bev and Cliff
and talking with the saints of old.

As much as we miss you
and wish we were there with you
For whatever reason
we have more work to do

Congratulations faithful servant
you have passed your final test
Enjoy your eternity
for you have earned your heavenly rest

About the Authors

Max Elliot Anderson works hard to develop books that will hold the interest of "reluctant" middle grade readers. From a lifetime of experience in film and video production, he brings visual excitement and heart-pounding action to his adventures and mysteries. http://middlegradeadventureandmystery.blogspot.com

Joye Atkinson was born in South Carolina. She has written poetry for 30 years, writing from personal experience. Her prayer is that the words God gives her will be a blessing to many. Her first book of poetry, *From the Heart,* is a recent publication. She is working on her second book. She declares, "To God be the glory for all he has done!"

Joe Bonsall, born and raised in Philadelphia, Pennsylvania, has been a member of The Oak Ridge Boys for more than 40 years. He and his singing partners — Duane Allen, William Lee Golden, and Richard Sterban — have won multiple awards, including five GRAMMYs˚, in several genres of music, from gospel to pop to country. The Oaks are members of the Country Music Hall of Fame, the Gospel Music Hall of Fame, and the Grand Ole Opry. They have sold more than 41 million records and charted more than 30 Top Ten singles.

Joe is also a bestselling author with more than 250,000 books sold. He and his wife, Mary, live with their five cats in Hendersonville, Tennessee. For relaxation, Joe retreats to his 350-acre farm on the Tennessee-Kentucky state line and can often be found on his John Deere tractor mowing fields — or sitting on his front porch and playing banjo. Josephsbonsall.com.

Shirley Brosius is the author of *Sisterhood of Faith: 365 Life-Changing Stories About Women Who Made a Difference,* a daily devotional book featuring historic and contemporary Christian women with messages from their lives. She enjoys writing, speaking and keeping up with her husband and two sons and their families; a daughter waits in heaven. Shirley also co-authored *Turning Guilt Trips into Joy Rides* along with two women with whom she shares a speaking ministry as Friends of the Heart.

Carlene Shuler Brown, a South Carolina Writer, has won numerous awards for her short stories, several of which are published in magazines.

In 2016 she won seventh place in the Writers Digest Annual Competition. She lives alone but enjoys spending time with her daughter's two cats, Cloud and Ceras.

Roger Bruner worked as a teacher, job counselor, and programmer analyst before retiring to pursue his dream of writing Christian fiction full-time. A guitarist and songwriter, he is active in his church choir, plays bass on the praise team, and plays guitar at the weekly nursing home ministry. Roger enjoys reading, web design, mission trips, photography, and spending time with his wonderful wife, Kathleen. He has nine published books: four in the missions-themed young adult *Altered Hearts* series; the series' coming-of-age prequel, *Rosa No-Name*; a speculative satire, *The Devil and Pastor Gus*; and three quirky romantic novels. He's also published two small books of shorter writings, *Yesterday's Blossoms* and *More of Yesterday's Blossoms*. Learn more about Roger and his writings at RogerBruner.com.

Penelope Carlevato was born in England and moved to the USA as a little girl. She was raised in an English home on the plains of South Dakota. She has been involved in the tea industry for over three decades, from having her own retail tea business, writing and speaking about tea to women's groups, historical organizations and business events. She is a tour leader for her annual "Taste of Britain" tea tours. Penelope is a Christian author and speaker and a member of the *Advanced Writers and Speakers Bureau* and the *Titanic Speakers Bureau*. She is a graduate of *Christian Leaders and Speakers* and a certified *Personality Trainer*. Her books include *Tea on the Titanic, First Class Etiquette and The Art of Afternoon Tea*. She is a contributing author for numerous compilation books.

She serves as a regular columnist for *Leading Hearts*, the award-winning magazine for Christian women in leadership, and the quarterly magazine, *Innovative Health*. She is a Registered Nurse and has written articles for medical and health and wellness magazines. A love of the Edwardian era and the traditions of that period provide the motivation for her books. She resides in Denver, Colorado with her husband, Norman. They have eleven grandchildren and one great-grandson.

Joann Claypoole is the award-winning author of *The Gardener's Helpers* (ages 5-8 Morgan James Pub. 2015). Current works in progress include children's chapter books, a Christmas speculative fantasy, middle grade, young adult, and fantasy novels, Christian women's living, and children's bedtime prayer books for ages 2-5. Visit her website at joannclaypoole.com She blogs at joannclaypoole.wordpress.com and has many inspirational stories featured in six of Yvonne Lehman's *Moments* books, and James Stuart Bell's *Jesus Talked To Me Today: True Stories of Children's Encounters with Angels, Miracles, and God.* Joann is a member of SCBWI and leads her local SCBWI writer critique group. She's a wife, mother of four sons, has four grandchildren, two crazy canines, and is a former salon/spa owner in sunny Central Florida. Connect with her on FB, Instagram, Linked In, Twitter @JoannClaypoole.

Wendy Dellinger writes to encourage women in the various seasons and challenges of life. Her work has appeared in *Chicken Soup for the Soul*, *God Allows U-Turns*, and various periodicals and curriculum projects. She makes her home in the beautiful Southwest with her husband and family.

Lola De Maci is a retired teacher whose stories have appeared in numerous editions of *Chicken Soup for the Soul, The Los Angeles Times, Sasee* and *Reminisce* magazines, as well as children's publications. Lola has a Master of Arts in education and English. She writes overlooking the San Bernardino Mountains. You may contact her at LDeMaci@aol.com

Diana Flegal is an avid reader who enjoys hanging out with and helping writers, as well as hiking in the mountains or kayaking the many lakes of her home state, North Carolina.

Gayle Fraser has an article in a Christmas anthology published by Grace Publishing and another in Little Cab Press. *The Dog Really Did That?* appeared in *Chicken Soup for the Soul*. She self-published *Dove*, a junior high girls' curriculum on self-identity and what Scripture says about being a young lady in Christ. She is editing and illustrating *Fairies' Tales*, a children's guide to Christian characteristics. She has developed *Grandma's Faithfulness Prayer Warriors*, a weekly prayer group for grandmothers who are encouraged to pray for Christian characteristics in their grandchildren. She developed a ministry, *Shhh, I'm a Secret Sister*, for women desiring to promote Christian characteristics and lifestyles for pre-teens through being a secret sister. Her children's books, *Mama Munk and Her Five Chipmunks* and *My Home Sweet Home*, which she wrote and illustrated, are available on Amazon. She wrote, illustrated, and self- published *Love Stories From Grandma's Heart,* for her grandchildren. Gayle took her granddaughter to Hungary with their church's youth group. She and her husband have smuggled Bibles into China, participated in the Billy Graham Crusade in Moscow, Russia, toured Israel. They live in Arizona.

Tommy Scott Gilmore, III is a speaker, teacher, motivational leader, and Executive Director of Changing Lives Ministry http://www.changinglivesministry.info/. Tommy is a graduate of Taylor University and Gordon Conwell Theological Seminary having a B.S. and a Master's in Education. He is published in *Decision Magazine, The Christian Athlete, The National Network of Youth Ministries, Single Minded, WNC Parent,* and contributed numerous articles to *Youth Specialties Encyclopedia for Youth Workers.* He wrote a Bible study in conjunction with music for Steven Curtis Chapman's "For the Sake of the Call." He is author of two training manuals, *A Comprehensive Pro Life Resource for Ministers, Politicians, Pro Life Workers,* and *Teachers,* and *Changing Lives Training Manual for Youth Workers* which has been used by numerous youth pastors in more than 29 states and missionaries in 7 countries. He has contributed several stories to Yvonne Lehman's compilations, *Christmas Moments, More Christmas Moments, Merry Christmas Moments, Divine Moments, Spoken Moments* and *Stupid Moments*. Other than being introduced to his best friend ever, Jesus Christ, the greatest joy of his life was to fall in love with 7 of the most beautiful women in the world. Beginning with the prettiest, his wife Sandra, they include his 3 daughters — Lindsey, Brittany and Meghan — followed by his granddaughters — Sarah and Victoria, and conclude with the most charming 4-legged creature (with a tail that never stops waging) — Miss Annie of Augusta Georgia and her brothers, Kirby and Mr. Finnegan.

Gigi Graham is the eldest daughter of Ruth and Billy Graham. She is the mother of seven grown children, grandmother to twenty grandchildren — so far — and seven greats. Gigi's experience as the daughter of a well-known evangelist, raising seven children, living in both the Middle East and Europe, has given her many resources for her writing and speaking ministry. She serves as Ambassador of the Billy Graham Training Center at The Cove in Asheville, North Carolina. Gigi is an award-winning author of several books including *Weather of the Heart, Currents of the Heart* and *A Quest for Serenity*. She divides her time between central Florida and the mountains of North Carolina and can be contacted through Ambassador Agency in Nashville, Tennessee.

Mary A. Hake, an Oregon native, is a freelance writer and editor with hundreds of published pieces in periodicals and compilation books. She often writes devotionals and created the content for *Creation: Thirteen 6-in-1 Lessons*. She has been a member of Oregon Christian Writers for more than thirty years and served on the board for twelve, including five as president. She has been married to Ted for forty-five years, and they have two adult daughters, who both teach at the college level. She has worked in a Christian bookstore and as a librarian, in addition to working in Christian schools before she began homeschooling her girls. Her desire is to encourage others.

Lydia E. Harris has been married to her college sweetheart, Milt for fifty-one years. They have two married children and five grandchildren aged 8 to 19. With a master's degree in home economics, Lydia creates and tests recipes with her grandchildren for *Pockets* and *Clubhouse* magazines. Her cookbook for grandparents and grandchildren is scheduled for publication in 2019. She also pens the column "A Cup of Tea with Lydia," which is published across the USA and Canada. No wonder her grandchildren call her "Grandma Tea." Lydia has also written hundreds of articles, book reviews, devotionals, and stories, and has contributed to 30 books. She is the author of the book, *Preparing My Heart for Grandparenting: For Grandparents at Any Stage of the Journey*.

Judith Victoria Hensley is an award winning teacher, author, newspaper columnist, and photographer from Harlan, Kentucky. She has been involved in over thirty book projects, and is currently developing a fourth book in the *Warrior Women* series: *Warrior Women, Victory on the Battlefront of the Mind*, which is a collection of stories from everyday women of various ages and many walks of life who share their personal life's challenges and God's love and intervention in their individual circumstances. Her latest book projects can be found on her Facebook page *Judith Victoria Hensley, Author* or by visiting her blog, *One Step Beyond the Door*. http://onestepbeyondthedoor.com/.

Helen L. Hoover and her husband are retired and live in Northwest Arkansas. Sewing, reading, knitting, traveling, pulling weeds from the flower gardens, and helping her husband with home repair occupy her time. Visits with their two living children, grandchildren and great-grandchildren are treasured. *Word Aflame Publishing, The Secret Place, Word Action Publication, The Quiet Hour, the Lutheran Digest, Light and Life Communications, Chicken Soup for the Soul,* and *Victory in Grace* have published her devotionals and personal articles.

Amanda Hughes holds a Master's Degree in Christian Education from Southwestern Baptist Theological Seminary. She serves as Outreach Director and 90-Day Study Director for the education foundation, Constituting America, and enjoys encouraging others through her writing on faith and freedom at her blog www.AmandaHughesWriter.com. Amanda is the author of *Who Wants to Be Free? Make Sure You Do!*. She lives in Washington, D.C. and is writing her second book.

Nancy Johnson, affectionately known and remembered as "Aunt Nancy," is a long-running radio personality in her hometown of Harlan, Kentucky. Her Bible Story program ran for over twenty years. She is a retired schoolteacher, Bible Study teacher, and Sunday school teacher.

Ann Knowles, author, editor, and teacher, wants the words she writes to touch hearts and make a difference in peoples' lives. She is a Gold Member of Christian Editors Network and a charter member of The Christian Proofreaders and Editors Network.

Ann enjoys speaking and teaching at churches, retreats, and writers conferences. She delights in mentoring new writers and working with college students whose first language is not English. Visit Ann at *Write Pathway Editorial Services — Where Writers an*d Editors Meet. www.writerpathway.com.

Yvonne Lehman is author of 59 novels and compiler of 10 non-fiction *Divine Moments* books, and serves as Acquisitions and Managing Editor of Candlelight Romance and Guiding Light Women's Fiction with Lighthouse Publishing of the Carolinas. She founded and directed the Blue Ridge Mountains Christian Writers Conference for 25 years and now directs the Blue Ridge "Autumn in the Mountains" Novelist Retreat. She earned a Master's Degree in English from Western Carolina

University and has taught English and Creative Writing on the college level. Her recent novel releases are *Secrets in Savannah* series (*The Caretaker's Son, Lessons in Love, Seeking Mr. Perfect, The Gift* and non-fiction compilation *Cool-inary Moments*. She periodically signs *Hearts that Survive — A Novel of the Titanic* at the Titanic Museum in Pigeon Forge, Tennessee. She blogs at www.christiansread.com and Novel Rocket. www.yvonnelehman.com — yvonnelehman3@gmail.com

Suzy Liggitt is a member of Northern Arizona Word Weavers. She grew up in Pasadena, California and lives in Cottonwood, Arizona with her husband, Jack. With their combined families, she and Jack have 8 children, 19 grandchildren and 6 great-grandchildren. She has been an Inspirational Speaker for over forty years for retreats, schools and churches. She worked on stage as a singer, actress and director. In addition she was Production Director in Christian Motion Picture and Associate Director of the *Something More* television show.

Lowell Lytle is the founder and president of Young American Showcase, a company based out of St. Petersburg, Florida that sent up to nine rock and roll groups per year throughout the United States and on limited engagements in other countries to reach youth for Jesus Christ. This ministry, which operated from 1970 to 1991, introduced tens of thousands of junior high and high school students to the Lord through groups collectively known as *Free Fare* and *Freedom Jam*. Prior to Young American Showcase, Lowell and his brother, Terry, built and operated two Christian drive-in theaters, one in Devil's Lake, Michigan, and the other in St. Petersburg, Florida, a ministry which led to his amazing connection to Billy Graham. Now in his late 80s, Lytle is currently artist in residence at the Titanic museum in Pigeon Forge, Tennessee, where he portrays E. J. Smith, captain of the ill-fated ship, and shares the gospel through the John Harper story, told to thousands of visitors each year. Lowell is also the oldest person to dive to the bottom of the North Atlantic to the salvage site of the Titanic, and is author of *Diving into the Deep*, his deeply moving and evangelistic true-life story. Following Billy Graham's example, Lowell is using every means possible to honor God and share the gospel with as many people as possible, as long as he possibly can. Email: Lowell.lytle@gmail.com.

Jayme H. Mansfield is an author, artist, and educator. Her award-winning novels, *Chasing the Butterfly* and *RUSH*, are book club favorites. *RUSH* received the 2018 Gold Medal Illumination Award for Christian Fiction and top awards in Colorado. Her stories weave artistic, visual imagery with compelling plots and captivating characters. Romance, nuggets from the past, and timeless, biblical truths provide the fiber to make her novels rich and memorable. Jayme and her husband have survived raising three hungry, hockey-playing sons. Currently, a very needy Golden Retriever rules the roost. When Jayme isn't writing, she teaches art to children and adults at her long-time art studio, Piggy Toes. Visit her at www.jaymehmansfield.com.

Diana Leagh Matthews writes, speaks and sings to bring glory to God. Her writings are published in numerous anthologies, including many *Divine Moments* books. In her day job, Diana is a Nationally Certified Activities Director for a busy nursing facility. She takes great joy in family, friends and soaking in the beautiful wonders and promises of God. She blogs about her faith and struggles on her website www.DianaLeaghMatthews.com, and family history at www.ALookThruTime.com.

Mary McQueen has served for many years as an ordained minister. She has lived in many states and completed studies in Europe. She and her husband Ken (also ordained) live and serve churches in Lincoln, Nebraska. They have five grown children. Mary has served as a police chaplain and is a facilitator in the Anti Violence Project inside prison walls. She and her husband are childbirth and gentle parenting instructors. She has coached and helped deliver a large number of healthy babies as part of her ministry. For more information, visit her blog at pastormcqueen.com or pastormaary.mac on Twitter.

Andrea Merrell is an associate editor with Christian Devotions Ministries and Lighthouse Publishing of the Carolinas. She is also a professional freelance editor and was a finalist for the 2016 Editor of the Year Award at BRMCWC. She teaches workshops at writers' conferences and has been published in numerous anthologies and online venues. Andrea is a graduate of Christian Communicators and a finalist in the 2015 USA Best Book Awards. She is the author of *Murder of a Manuscript, Praying for the Prodigal,* and *Marriage: Make It or Break It*. For more information, visit www.AndreaMerrell.com or www.TheWriteEditing.com.

Lynn Mosher has a deep passion to share her devotions and inspirational stories, fulfilling God's call on her life to encourage others and glorify the Lord. She is published in the books: *Entering the God of Wholeness, Ya Know What I'm Say'n,* and *Overwhelmed: 31 Stories from M.O.M.* She contributes to sites and magazines including *Secret Place, Comfort Café, Internet Café, Novel Rocket, High Calling, CrossRoads,* and *Author Culture.* Lynn is a monthly columnist for online and print venues including: *TheMOMInitiative.com, LivingBetterat50+, Ruby for Women, Daily Signs of Hope, Lift Up Your Day for Women, The Consilium* and *Grace&Faith4U.* Her first book is in the process of being published and she is working on her second book. She also writes twice weekly on her website: LynnMosher.com.

Vicki H. Moss is Contributing Editor for *Southern Writers Magazine* and past Editor-at-Large. A columnist for the *American Daily Herald,* she's also a poet, author of *How to Write for Kids' Magazines* and *Writing with Voice,* a Precept Ministries leader and a Christian Communicators graduate. She has written for *Hopscotch* and *Boy's Quest* magazines for the last decade in addition to being published in *Christmas Moments, Divine Moments* and *Precocious Moments,* SouthWest Writers' *Sage, Country Woman, In the City, Borderlines,* Scotland's *Thistle Blower,* and *I Believe in Heaven.* She was selected to be a presenter of her fiction and creative nonfiction short stories for three conferences in a row at the Southern Women Writers Conference held at Rome, Georgia's Berry College. Vicki is also a speaker and on faculty for writers conferences. For more information visit livingwaterfiction.com.

Patricia Luellen Nicholas is an award-winning author who writes Bible studies, devotions, articles, a blog and contemporary fiction. She has worked for the Billy Graham Evangelistic Association at The Cove in Asheville North Carolina for many years in several different capacities. She discovered the true meaning of God's grace when her grief journey began with the deaths of her husband Dave Nicholas, and her father Bill Luellen. Her heart is to share her love of Jesus with others. Her passion is in the study of God's word, and teaching others how to study for themselves. Her ministry is helping others who have also experienced loss. Patty is the mother of two beautiful grown daughters and Nana of two grandchildren. She lives in the mountains of North Carolina with her dog, Stella.

Karen Lynn Nolan is a writer, actress, musician, artist, Kentucky mountain storyteller, and mom. Her love of mystery and suspense means she usually includes a dead body in anything she writes. Her first Appalachian novel releases in late 2018. Karen, an award-winning writer, has pieces included in several anthologies. Her mission as she writes about her journey through natural disasters, chronic illness, depression, homelessness, several near-death experiences, late-life divorce, and financial ruin is to show others how to find joy during adversity.

Diane H. Pitts encourages others through writing. Diane's day job is in the healing art of physical therapy. For the last ten years she has cared for elderly parents and hopes to make this a writing wellspring. She and her husband live on Alabama's Gulf Coast. Her latest venture was as contributing author to the landmark textbook *Lifespan Neurorehabilitation*.

Kim Peterson, as a child, disappeared up her cherry trees with a good book and a thermos of juice. As an adult, her love for the written word is expressed through mentoring aspiring writers online at Taylor University and previously as Associate Faculty in Writing at Bethel College. As a freelance writer, editor, and conference speaker, her writing has appeared in various anthologies, including *Chicken Soup for the Caregiver's Soul* and *Rocking Chair Reader: Family Gatherings*. Her articles and book reviews have been published in local newspapers and in magazines including *Christian Market, Encounter, The Secret Place,* and *Seek*, among others.

Debbie M. Presnell is an author, speaker, and Bible study teacher. Prior to writing and teaching Bible studies, she spent 30 years in higher education where she trained future teachers — and she admits this was a dream profession! Debbie facilitates an online Bible study on Facebook and teaches Bible study in her church. She has written *Shine! Radiating the Love of God,* a Bible study designed for teens ages 13-18. Her women's Bible study, *Shine On!,* and devotional, *Shining Through the Psalms,* are scheduled for release in 2018. Several of her articles appear in the *Divine Moments* series. She blogs and brings regular inspirational nuggets on her Facebook page: ShineEveryDayNC. In addition to *writing, she* loves encouraging other woman and feels honored when God allows her the opportunity to share His Word at women's events. Debbie is married, has three adult children, and an eight-year old granddaughter. She camps, rides her bike and walks, and loves the mountains and the beach. Visit her website at www.debbiepresnell.com; email her at: debpres@yahoo.com.

Colleen L. Reece describes herself as an ordinary person with an extraordinary God. Raised in a home without electricity or running water but filled with love for God and family, Colleen learned to read by kerosene lamplight and dreamed of someday writing a book. God has multiplied her "someday" book into *150 Books You Can Trust*, with six million copies sold.

Fred Robinson, Jr. was born and grew up in the beautiful, historic town of Aberdeen, Mississippi. His parents, Viola and Fred Robinson, were faithful in church attendance and their children, Fred, Jr. and Viola Ann, always joined them in worship. While both children took piano lessons, their grandparents, H.B. and Mertie Robinson, took them to gospel singings and music conventions where they both came to love gospel music and its importance in worship. Beginning in 1975, Fred, Jr. was a member of the First Baptist Church Sanctuary Choir in Jackson, Mississippi, for ten consecutive years. This choir was asked to participate in the Billy Graham Crusade Choir in May 1975.

Karen Sawyer is a writer whose work has appeared in *Loving Moments, Precious, Precocious Moments, Wounded Women of the Bible, The Secret Place Devotional, Girlfriend 2 Girlfriend* magazine, and *MONTROSE ANYTIME magazine*. Her guest blog posts have been in *Mother Inferior* and *Unsent Letters*. She has contributed numerous articles to *ehow,* and Demand Media's other web-based sites. She taught elementary school for seven years before her children, now grown, were born. Karen resides in Austin, Texas with her husband.

Cindy Sproles is author of the best-selling books, *Mercy's Rain* and *Liar's Winter*. Her articles appear in several of the *Divine Moments* series. She is the cofounder of Christian Devotions Ministries and the Executive Editor of www.christiandevotions.us and www.inspireafire.com. Cindy is the acquisitions editor for *SonRise Books* and *Straight Street Books*, imprints of Lighthouse Publishing of the Carolinas. She teaches at writers conferences and women's conferences nationwide. Visit Cindy at www.cindysproles.com

Nate Stevens is a "missionary kid" who grew up in a Christian home and church. He has enjoyed a 36-year banking career in a variety of leadership roles. He is the author of *Matched 4 Life* and *Deck Time with Jesus* as well as a contributing author on several of the books in the Moments series (*Divine Moments, Spoken Moments, Christmas Moments*). He writes online devotions for ChristianDevotions.us and *SingleMatters.com* as well as articles for several other publications. He is a popular speaker and teacher at conferences, seminars and Bible study groups, speaking on a wide variety of topics. Nate lives near Charlotte, North Carolina, with his beautiful wife, Karen, and is a proud dad of two awesome kids, Melissa and Mitchell.

Barb Suiter enjoys sharing spiritual truths learned from nature, a blessed 54-year-marriage, and everyday events through her blog: *ajourneytonow.me*. Pastor's wife, writer, Bible teacher, former missionary in Western Europe, grandmother of 13, Barb also writes for *ChristiansDevotions.com* and is published in a *Moments* book. She and her husband Tom live in Lawrenceburg, Tennessee where she doesn't know whether to "weed or write."

Audrey Tyler grew up in a Christian home and church. She is a contributing writer for her church newsletter, *Samaria Today*. She is published in *Refresh Bible Study Magazine* and in two of the *Divine Moments* series: *Spoken Moments* and *Stupid Moments*. Audrey lives in South Carolina with her husband.

Beverly Varnado is an author, screenwriter, blogger and artist. Her newest books are *Faith in the Fashion District,* the story of how one woman's life on Seventh Avenue launched a lifetime in ministry, and a novel, *The Key to Everything*. She has a screenplay under option, which was a finalist for the prestigious Kairos Prize in Screenwriting. She has contributed to several anthologies, print magazines, and online sites and has two other novels in print, *Give My Love to the Chestnut Trees* and *Home to Currahee*. She is always working on a new painting and had fun writing and editing the blog *One Old Dawg: mostly true Bulldog lore* with her husband, Jerry, a former college football player. Visit her on her weekly blog, *One Ringing*

Bell: peals of words on faith, living, writing, and art. OneRingingBell.blogspot.com or her website, www.BeverlyVarnado.com.

Debra DuPree Williams is an award-winning author whose work has appeared in *Stupid Moments, Additional Christmas Moments,* Michelle Medlock Adams' *Love and Care for the One and Only You,* in addition to other publications. When she isn't writing, you will likely find her chasing an elusive ancestor, either through online sources or in country graveyards. Debbie is a classically-trained lyric coloratura soprano whose first love is southern gospel. She has been married forever to the best man on earth, is the mother of four sons, mother-in-law of one extraordinary daughter-of-her-heart, and DD to the two most-beautiful and talented young ladies ever. Debbie divides her time between North Carolina and Florida.

Dr. Rhett H. Wilson, Sr. is an award-winning freelance writer who blogs at www.rhettwilson.blogspot.com. Rhett has pastored churches in Kentucky and South Carolina and taught Bible as an adjunct professor of Christianity at Anderson University. He and his family live in upstate South Carolina. The Wilsons like playing board games and exploring waterfalls, and they look forward to March Madness every year. For fun, he reads legal thrillers and listens to Broadway, country, and symphony music.

Ann Brubaker Greenleaf Wirtz, public speaker and group study leader, is the author of both *Hand of Mercy* and the Bible study that accompanies her new release. Ann won the Willie Parker Peace History Book Award from the North Carolina Society of Historians for her book *The Henderson County Curb Market*. Her first book, *Sorrow Answered*, was published in 2006. She was published in *More Christmas Moments, Chicken Soup for the Soul Christmas*, and locally in the *Times-News*, where she has written over 100 articles. She writes a nostalgic remembrance for *The Pulse* each December, featuring her childhood in Webster Groves, Missouri. Ann is the mother of one very dear son and daughter-in-law, and the grandmother of two delightful grandchildren, a girl and a boy. She is married to her beloved Patrick, and they reside in Hendersonville, North Carolina.

www.ingramcontent.com/pod-product-compliance
Lightning Source LLC
Chambersburg PA
CBHW042128160426
43198CB00021B/2945